Gitanerias

The Essence of Flamenco

3

Tony Bryant

4

Dedicated to Javier

In memory of Anita and Hugo

CONTENTS

ACKNOWLEDGEMENTS

Once again I find myself confronted with the difficult task of deciding who first to start with, when producing the necessary acknowledgments of those who have helped with this work.

The input and help came from varying sources and whilst some of these people gave me plentiful information and content for this book; others were simply caught in a moment of sheer bliss, but that fleeting few seconds of genius was as valued as any other input I received.

Many institutions helped with varying information and statistics, and these include the *Ayuntamiento de Utrera* - whose help was monumental concerning Utrera's past history: as well I must acknowledge the huge amount of assistance that I received from the staff of the municipal library in Utrera.

The brotherhood of the gypsies of Utrera, and the churches of Santiago el Mayor, and Santa Maria de la Mesa, must also be credited for information concerning *Semana Santa* and Utrera's religious history.

Of the people; well, this is where the problem begins, because I hold a very special place in my heart for the people of Utrera, and each one that has befriended me, has demonstrated open-handedness and camaraderie in abundance.

For this reason I feel that there is no need to list them in this section because they have each been recognized within the pages of this book.

All that needs to be said is that I am deeply grateful, and profoundly indebted, to the gypsies of Utrera once again.

Viva Utrera!

GITANERIAS; THE ART OF PERFORMING FLAMENCO WITH THE ZEST OF THE GYPSIES

Gitanerias is a word that will conjure many images for those familiar with the gypsies of Andalusia, and it is a word that has a much deeper meaning in the world of flamenco, than the depiction one will find in the Spanish dictionary.

Cajolery, flattery, deceit, and gypsy-like is how this word is translated, but when used with regards to flamenco, gitanerias means gitanerias; a little bit of Gypsy magic that separates them from the *gacho*, or non-gypsy, flamencos.

The nearest accurate translation would be 'gypsyism', which refers to the arts, habits and practices of being a Gypsy, but even this does not suffice the true meaning of gitanerias; for this word is what best describes the gypsies doing what only they can do.

9

It is that little flick of the wrist, or the raising of the eyebrow and the contortion of the face that sets them apart, and no matter what age, shape or size, they appear to possess a natural affinity with rhythm that makes their performance far more spellbinding than the academically trained performers.

The gypsies are the very essence of flamenco, and yet we must remember that flamenco is not solely a style of music and dance; it is phenomenon that has many ingredients, and for it to be at its most appreciable, it must contain a little 'gitanerias'.

Dormant Charm

The majority of towns and villages in the lower region of Andalusia have shared a similar existence over the years and although much of Spain has changed considerably since Franco's demise; many of the smaller villages still adhere to a very traditional way of living.

In view of the fact that Franco had first refused help or influence from the western world after his victory in 1939, Spain's doors remained tightly shut to what was happening in the rest of Europe and America.

At the dawn of the 1950s, most of Europe had started to recover from the effects of the Second World War and many countries began to prosper both commercially and culturally.

11

Franco's Spain was, of course, an exception: the lousy economy, the iron-fist of martial law, and Catholicism kept Spain locked in an era of totalitarianism.

Franco established policies that were highly favourable to the Catholic Church - the only legal state religion - like banning civil marriages, making divorce illegal and religious education compulsory in schools.

Spanish law discriminated strongly against married women and under the *permiso marital,* they were prohibited from almost all economic activities without the permission of their husband.

Franco saw himself as the one designated to save Spain from the chaos and instability of democracy, and until his death in 1975, he remained the ultimate source of legitimate authority.

Yet Franco was keen to impress the world's democratic powers after the Allied victory in 1945, so measures were implemented to make his regime appear less arbitrary in order to give it a facade of democracy.

However, as the 1940s came to an end amidst agricultural imbalances, labour unrest and near famine, the need for raw materials and credit forced Franco to make some connection with the west.

Franco's rule was harsh to say the least and even though the canons of his regime would slacken in later years, he held a firm grip on his country and its people throughout his supremacy.

Carnivals and ferias were banned, as were large gatherings of people in public places, and his regime enforced strict curfew rules which forbid people to be on the streets after dark without due reason.

But the average Andalusian is strong and determined and although many lived in abysmal conditions, their simple lust for life somehow kept them afloat.

The Andalusians certainly have a penchant for pleasure and they will enjoy the most wonderful of *fiestas* with the minimum of preparation.

A quiet beer in a small bar can turn into the most enduring fiesta, and the music and dance, or entertainment in whatever form, is supplied by whoever is in attendance. This type of fiesta may last for just a few hours, or continue well into the next day!

However, in Franco's culturally isolated Spain, wild boisterous flamenco sessions were not tolerated, which was quite ironic, because at the end of the 1950s, he nationalized flamenco in a bid to attract tourism and vital foreign currency.

The average Andalusian did not own a television or a telephone and, with the exception of the highly censored press, their first contact with what was happening in the west arrived with the Americans.

Spain was the only major Western European country excluded from the Marshall Plan because it did not overtly participate in WW11.

After the war, Spain pursued a policy of self-sufficiency, although with little success, and fortunately, the United States finally embraced Spain as an ally[1].

In 1953, America was given permission to use two air-force bases in Andalusia and this was to be the beginning of events that would alter the life style of many Andalusians. Along with audacious American fashion, came rock and roll, and many young Spaniards got a taste for the life-style that went with it. The contemporary style of living that was taking place in the rest of Europe slowly seeped into Andalusia, and with it, hordes of foreigners in search one of Andalusia's stately treasures: flamenco.

Unfortunately, for the foreigners who came in search of flamenco *falsettas*, the young Andalusian guitarists were

14

---

[1] With the escalation of the Cold War, and Franco's aggressive anti-communist policies, America accepted Spain as an ally in 1951

more interested in the extraordinary new sounds of the copious supply of contemporary American musicians.

Numerous Americans and Europeans travelled to the small-impoverished agricultural towns in Andalusia to seek the knowledge of guitarists like Diego del Gastor; but once there they quickly realized that 'studying flamenco' is more than simply learning complicated guitar licks. The learning process requires immersing oneself in a different day-to-day social culture and with that, one learns by listening to, and observing what people do with, and say about, this very complex art.

This was an era when the main mode of transport would have been a horse or mule and the land was still worked by beasts of burden: it was also a time when people would sing as they went about their daily chores. Sadly, with the introduction of mechanical farm machinery and the incursion of the motor car, the heavenly sound of singing in the open air has been virtually erased from Andalusia.

The turbulence of modernisation has been one of the key factors in the demise of the flamenco way of life, and when Franco allowed the 20th century into Spain, he let out much of the charm that had lain dormant for hundreds of years.

Towards the end of Franco's dictatorship and the eventual return to democracy, the changes in social values and everyday Spanish life were extensive.

The wheels of the tourist industry that Franco had instigated were destroying the charm of the coastal fishing villages and the tranquil hilltop towns.

Of course, together with the destruction of Andalusia came the distortion of much of its cultural assets and traditions: flamenco, for example, became a kitsch form of tourist entertainment and it bore no resemblance, what so ever, to the time-honoured art of the gypsies.

Much of the traditional flamenco way of life has disappeared in the turmoil of the twenty-first century, but there are certain enclaves where a little of this antiquated attractiveness still exists.

Although Seville is one of the most favourite foreign tourist destinations, the surrounding towns of Utrera, Lebrija and Morón de la Frontera are way off the average tourist's route and so they have retained much of that old village-life charm.

The attitude of the people has not changed either and although they are not unknowing of foreign visitors, they have not altered their traditions and lifestyles in order to satisfy them.

The ambience of these quaint towns is often somewhat unperturbed and when one strolls around the tiny streets of Utrera, one is confronted with dream-like beauty.

Unfortunately, the water vendor no longer pulls his heavy wooden cart through the town, fresh bread is not delivered by bicycle, milk is not collected by churn, and horse-drawn taxis have vanished. Nevertheless, the corner shop is still the meeting point for local gossip and chitchat, the barbershop is still the gentlemen's club, the town square is still the epitome of social activity, and community spirit is thriving.

The present style of life and the daily work routines of the people in the major cities of Spain are not too different to any other in Europe, but in the southern-most part of Andalusia, local fiestas and colourful celebrations constantly interrupt routine.

The worries and strains of life are tossed to one side during the *feria* and any debts that may be mounting will be ignored in order to remunerate the following days of fiesta.

Even in times of financial crisis, when governments and local councils are forced to drastically cut their spending to a bare minimum; there always seem to be plentiful money for times of celebration.

This is most evident during the ferias in Andalusia, and although most towns and villages have now moderated the length of this annual cascade of intemperance; the money that is lavished on, and at, them is astronomical.

Much the same can be said of the gargantuan spending that takes place during Semana Santa, when Andalusians will disburse more money during a few days of piety, than they will perhaps earn in a month.

Although Andalusians are a nation of determinedly hard grafters, essentially, they are one that lives to be happy, and not one that exists merely to survive.

One of the great traditional values that still exists in Spain, especially Andalusia, is that of the family togetherness; something that is fast disappearing from England.

18

The family fiesta is a gathering of life and an explosion of noise, during which, food will arrive in a constant flow and wine in a limitless one.

The conversation will bounce around the room in constant competition and inevitably, once the wine has produced the required effect, the fiesta will progress.

There is no sight more pleasing than that of an ageing grandmother, with her skirt hitched above her knee, who performs a quick dance routine that is so raw it hurts.

The most amazing part of it all, however, is the sheer self-enjoyment of the whole procedure, because it is not done to impress, but simply, to enjoy.

A SEDUCTIVE MAGNETISM

One of my first encounters with flamenco happened many years ago in a commercial flamenco *tablao* on the Costa del Sol. I soon began to realize that what I had witnessed on that night was not the most authentic form of this art, but it was, if I remember correctly, the night that started an infectious obsession with Andalusia that has since overwhelmed my life.

It is an oft-voiced opinion that Andalusia, and especially its flamenco, exude a seductive capacity that will infect or seduce anyone who gets too close.
I can declare that this belief has some bearing, because today, many years after this early encounter, my enthusiasm for Andalusian tradition has practically engulfed me.

A Gypsy singer once warned me to be careful, because flamenco, said he, is like another world and once you have entered it you will never return.
He was of course referring to the orthodox style and not the, sometimes absurd, tourist-tablao style of flamenco that is often passed off as 'authentic Gypsy art'

My fascinations lead me on a journey around Andalusia in search of the more traditional side of this wonderful art and it was this expedition that acquainted me with so many different aspects of the Andalusian way of living.

It is no easy task to reveal the mysteries that shroud this wonderful area of southern Spain, and one must try to understand that flamenco is not just a style of music; it is a complex cultural way of life that requires a deep understanding.

Once a small agricultural town, Utrera has an age-old flamenco essence that distinguishes it from all others, and their flamenco has been caringly nurtured and it is as good today as it's ever been.

Famed for its Gypsy *juergas* that once attracted flamencos[2] from all parts of Andalusia, Utrera is, without doubt, one of the most 'flamenco' enclaves of them all.

The surrounding country side is profuse with blood-red poppies and line upon line of golden sunflowers basking in the sweltering heat.

---

[2] The word flamenco refers to both the music and the people that are involved with it, and I have used the term in both contexts throughout this book.

Olive and almond groves stand silent and motionless in the cracked and scorched soil, and the continual hum of the tree-hoppers is so often the only sound one hears.

Storks nest high on the towers of crumbling monasteries and castles, and the sight of these regal creatures gliding overhead is a magnificent and quite up-lifting vision.

The history of Utrera is particularly interesting and is by no means limited to flamenco, because it is a town with an illustrious past.

The grand palatial-homes and churches that are nestled amongst the small streets are a constant reminder of the many different periods that have made this town so intimately special, and one cannot fail to succumb to the antiquated charm of the village-type ambience.

Ernest Hemingway once declared, 'if a man feels more at home outside of where he was born, then that is where he is meant to be'.

Utrera has definitely become my home from home, and it is a town that I have grown to love and greatly admire, and even though it was indeed the flamenco that I first came in search of; it is the seductive magnetism of this small Gypsy enclave that has infatuated me beyond conviction.

My association with the people of Utrera has given me the opportunity to witness a way of life that far exceeds anything I have ever experienced before. They opened a door that led to another sphere where a deep awareness of flamenco was abounding, and the simple appreciation of life was foremost.

During the research for a previous project, which is based on the genealogy of Fernando 'El Pinini', I was invited into the homes and personal lives of many of his descendants. My presence was often requested at birthday or anniversary celebrations, communion and baptism ceremonies, and as well, the habitual festivities that take place during the feria, Semana Santa and the numerous other occasions of celebration.

I was also introduced to many aspects of their ways and beliefs, like their devotion to the town's patron Saint, *La Virgen de la Consolacíon*, their attitude concerning life and death, and their incessant need for the flamenco way of living.

I gained access to areas of their lives that I could not have dreamed possible and many of these people have since become treasured and honorable friends.

This book is largely based on my own personal experiences in, and impressions of, Utrera.

Utrera has always been important as far as flamenco is concerned, and we are forever reminded of past masters like Tio Benito, El Perrate, Bambino and La Fernanda de Utrera.

One of the things that have amazed me is the fact that the descendants of this huge flamenco clan are continuing with the legacy, and although we must never forget the art of past masters, we must surely take notice of those who are maintaining Utrera's flamenco heritage.

It is often said that the flamenco way of life is fast disappearing from Andalusia, and to a certain extent this is true, but there are places, like Utrera, where this hereditary way of existence will no doubt continue for eternity.

Yo vengo de Utrera is a phrase that is said with great pride and self-esteem, and it is certainly one of the best characteristics a flamenco can possess[3].

---

[3] Yo vengo de Utrera – I come from Utrera!

THE ROAD TO UTRERA

I remember my first visit to Utrera with much affection, because I was overcome with elation and, although I was soaked to the bone by the time I had walked the short distance from the train station to the centre, I knew that this was to be the beginning of a long and passionate association with the town.

October is rain season and the enormous charcoal-black clouds that sagged over Utrera on this day would soon empty onto the town like a monsoon.

Calle Nueva was the first place on my list because many of the town's flamenco performers were born, or had lived, there during Utrera's golden flamenco years, but my eagerness was assailed by the perpetual driving rain that pierced my face like thousands of tiny needles.

I headed to the first open bar, the *Peña Betica*, which is in front of the old fountain in the very centre of the town.

This bar is a football peña dedicated to *Real Betis FC* and it is a place where locals gather to speculate about forth coming games or revel over recent triumphs.

My atrocious attempt to converse in Spanish prompted the ashen-faced bar tender to continue with his duties as if I was not actually there.

Luckily, for me, one of the customers took over the conversation and instructed the barmen as to what it was I had actually ordered. He then went on to ask me what I was doing in Utrera on such a day; was I lost?

I explained that, amongst other things, I was in search of the monument of La Fernanda and La Bernarda de Utrera.

He informed me that the life-size bronze statue was just a short distance from the bar, and he then began to enlighten me of all the other places I should see if I was interested in Utrera's flamenco history.

It was obvious that the rain had set in for the duration of the day and so, after my caffeine injection, and much speculation from a few old guys in the bar, I opened my umbrella and preceded in the direction I had been given.

This first encounter with Utrera happened back in October of 2003 and since this initial experience I have had so many wonderful occasions in the town.

My interest with Utrera started with a fascination of two Gypsy sisters whose names dominated the art of flamenco, and they are probably the most recognized female singers in the history of flamenco to date.

It was the deathly, haunting cry of La Fernanda de Utrera that first drew me to the town and even though she passed away in 2006, her presence is forever felt, simply because the town still mourns her today.

Although a relative amount of the twenty-first century has arrived in Utrera, much of its antediluvian life-style is still evident, and from the minute one arrives in the town, this primordial ambience will engulf you.

The station's café-bar has an aged charm and, even though it is relatively plain looking, it is not the typical rail-road hole that often has less appeal than the station's waiting room.

This bar was once the congregational point of the *cocheros*; the fabulous horse-drawn carriages with brass lamps and swish leather seats that disappeared from the streets of Utrera in 1977. Today, they are only seen during the feria week, and the sound of trotting hooves has often dragged me from a much-needed siesta during this week of continual body abuse.

The heart of the town is the Plaza Altozano, yet this area has undergone numerous changes at the hands of town planners since the nineteenth century and much of the charm of this square has been razed. Unfortunately, one of the squares most treasured monuments was demolished during alterations in 1963 and this act is still considered an architectural disaster by many of the locals.

The old ayuntamiento building, with its glorious clock and vaulted bell-tower, was destroyed to make way for the bland looking Central Bank building.

This was once the most picturesque corner of the plaza and the first photographic evidence of this splendid clock- tower was taken around 1880: this picture shows the building adjoining the *Puerta de Sevilla*, one of the medieval arched gateways that led in to the square.

The most prevalent image of Utrera is the huge *Iglesia de Santiago el Mayor*; a fifteenth century gothic master-piece that's robust tower and chapel dome can be seen from miles away.

Upwardly projecting at lower altitudes there are a number of interesting baroque domes decorated with the mosaic ceramic tiles so traditional of Andalusian temples. One of Utrera's resident Storks has taken a shine to this church and her twiggy nest perches clumsily on the edge of the decorative bell-tower.

The church is located in the highest part of the town and the quiet cobbled streets that lead down into the centre of Utrera are a maze of ramshackle houses flanked by three-storey palatial homes.

Some of the buildings are nothing more than crumbling facades propped upright with huge iron girders that are bolted to the pavement: others are newly renovated and look somewhat striking in comparison to the timeworn abodes that adjoin them.

One of the aspects I like most about Utrera, as with most of Andalusia, is its houses, and although you may admire the traditional house with its white-plastered architectural charm, one seldom gets any idea of what lays within.

Every house will almost certainly contain a patio, and it is here where the occupants will entertain friends, or simply relax with their family.

The patio is the heart of the home and these elegantly decorated spaces allows fresh air to circulate and create an intimate space within a property, and this is usually the most picturesque part of the home.

The patio is decorated with vibrant mosaic tiles, and crammed with pots of jasmine, geranium, and various cacti and leafy plants, and most will have a small fountain to add to the sense of peace and serenity that these spaces emit.

It is usual for the house to be built around the patio and so any noise or celebration is virtually inaudible from outside; hence they are a favorite space in which to hold a fiesta.

The patio will lead to the *azotea*, or the flat roof-top, where one gets birds eye views of the area, and I have spent many a night marveling at the beauty of Utrera at sunset, and, indeed, at sunrise.

Utrera is crammed with historic buildings and one splendid piece of the towns archaic past is the *Arco de Villa;* a 14th century arch that was once part of the old defensive wall that surrounded Utrera. It was one of four gateways that corresponded to the cardinal points of the town, although this is the only one of the four that remains today.

Another part of the characteristic landscape of Utrera, which can be seen from most parts of the town, is the bell-tower of the *Iglesia Santa Maria de la Mesa*; a massive gothic and renaissance bulk of a church that stands on the site of an old mosque. There are not many details concerning Utrera's Islamic past, and the first data with historical accuracy comes from the *reconquista* in the thirteenth century.[4]

The residential back streets of Utrera are in a state of tranquillity at all times, and this serene environment is only interrupted by the clanging of the church bells or the buzzing exhaust of a scooter.

The town takes on a rather special tenor throughout autumn when one is able to see the varying shades of the buildings without the glare of the blazing sun obscuring the landscape. The clouds create a most dazzling array of colour, especially in the early evening when the sky is filled with an orange tint, which illuminates the tops of the old buildings that sprout up from the tiny streets in an array of attractiveness.

33

---

[4]It is also unclear as to when the town was first christened with the name of Utrera, although it has been called so since at least the X111 century.

The aroma of roasted chestnuts fills the air in the plaza, a sign that winter is well and truly on its way, and the chatter of a thousand birds replaces the cyclical hum of the *cigarras*.[5]

One of the best aspects of the Andalusian way of living is the love of the outdoors, and other than in times of extreme weather, this is where they will normally be found.

The streets come alive around five in the afternoon and the once tranquil atmosphere is replaced by the hubbub of the residents who flock to the plaza in droves.

The plaza is the nerve centre of the town and daily life seems to revolve around the many bars and cafes that are located there.

The shrill of the birds and the children, and the whirl of mopeds, fills the air, yet there is a muted calmness that makes one feel incredibly relaxed.

There were once numerous barbershops in Utrera, which also served as a cultural *tertulia,* and the men would congregate in them to air their views and opinions. The barber was a good source of information concerning anything to do with the

---

[5]The name of this insect is a direct derivation of the Latin *cicada* meaning 'tree cricket'.

town simply because he was engaged in polite conversation on a daily basis.

Only one of these old barbers still exists in the square today and although the name has not been changed since the 19th century, it has been renovated and modernized and has lost much of the charm of the old establishment that once stood here.

Many of the old businesses like the cobblers, the ironmongers and the watch-smith have long gone, but a few of the buildings have kept their original facades, and a little of their charm.

The town once abounded with characters like Vega el Panadero; the local baker who would ride his iron framed tricycle along the high-curbed backstreets, selling freshly baked bread from the pannier-box of his archaic pedal-driven vehicle.

Sadly, many of these archetypical characters have long departed these streets, although there are still a few who seem to have stepped straight from the sepia post-card image of Andalusia.

Nearly all of Utrera's luminaries are just every-day people whose character and personage has been stamped into the town's history. Many of the town's famed flamenco performers were not professional artistes; instead, they earned their crust as butchers, labourers and farmhands.

My early visits to the town were uneventful, because I was a stranger and somewhat alienated, and so I would wander aimlessly looking for the monuments and plaques relevant to the Utrera's flamenco hierarchy.

In next to no time however, my jaunts would become anything but run of the mill research, because I soon began to make contacts that would open up a sprawling avenue of help and assistance. Today when I visit, a simple stroll through the main plaza can take up half the morning, and I am constantly stopped, or greeted, by relatives of one of the town's most talked about singers – Fernando Peña Soto.

El Pinini, the name by which Fernando is affectionately remembered, was born in the neighbouring town of Lebrija in 1863, but had spent nearly his entire life in Utrera.

Fernando's father had moved his family to Utrera in 1871 and it was in the streets of this town that the legend of El Pinini was cultivated.

El Pinini was a humble butcher that created a personal style of *cantina,* a lively style of flamenco song popular in this area, and yet he was further recognized for his drunken antics in the bars and streets of Utrera.

He was one of four children; one girl and three boys. His sister Inés never married, but El Pinini and his two brothers, Manuel and Juan, were to produce the roots of a family tree whose branches would bear many of the most respected flamenco performers of the twentieth century.

I was constantly advised to be careful when dabbling with the legend of El Pinini, because the roots and branches of his family are so entangled and matted, it would for sure send me insane!

Although I was driven to despair whilst researching El Pinini's seemingly interminable family line, it was the solidarity of the people and the attractiveness of the town that made it so all worthwhile.

Tomás de Perrate was the first person I made contact with and it was he that began to open doors that would take me deep into the abyss of his illustrious family.

Son of the great El Perrate de Utrera and grandson of the legendary Manuel Torre, Tomás is one of today's most prominent flamenco singers. With his help, this huge labyrinth of Gypsy lineage slowly started to make sense and he informed me of who best to talk to, with regards to the different sections of this mammoth genealogical tree.[6]

José Fernández - a great great-grandson of Pinini - was another acquaintance that I made in the early stages of my research.

He is from the line of the celebrated Miguel El Funi; one of the parts of the family tree that I was having difficulty with at the time.

Our first meeting was held in the *Bodegas Doña Juana* in Utrera and it was during this meeting that José became the first person to see the hand-written family tree whilst it was still a work in progress. He wittily inquired where I had started with such a tedious task, especially considering that El Pinini's grandchildren and great-grandchildren alone would surpass three-hundred people.

This is to mention nothing of the numerous marriage lines that link this family with so many renowned flamenco clans of the area.

---

[6]The family of El Perrate are not blood relatives of El Pinini, but the two families are intertwined through numerous liaisons.

Luis el Marquesito was another person who showed so much interest in the book that I was writing, and he even offered to write the prologue; an offer that I willingly accepted.

Our first introduction came during the feria in Utrera and, because of him, I quickly found myself invited into the company of many of Utrera's finest Gypsy flamencos.

Manolito de Angustias, one of today's most prominent flamenco singers, is another person whom I have come to know and admire, and he provided me with information concerning many aspects of life in Utrera, and he shared his profound understanding regarding the world of the bullfight.

Even though Manolito makes his living as a professional singer, he declares that his passion for the bull is far greater than his love of singing.

Too old, at forty-three, to become a professional matador, Manolito contents hisself with regular trips to a local ranch called *Guardiola*, where he is allowed access to the private bullring.

Manolito, nephew of the late Bambino, made his first recording on an old cassette machine in his bedroom and today is he one of Utrera's most foremost singers.

As a child, he would hang out in the bar owned by his uncle Diego Charmona, and it was here that he would learn the basics of flamenco singing, and it was also a period that nurtured his love of bullfighting.

Manolito, born in Utrera in 1970, is the son of José Alonso Rodriguez, a non-gypsy, only child, who had no flamenco background: his mother, Angustias Jiménez Cerezo, is the daugter of a legendary singer called Manuel Jiménez Ramirez, alias Manuel de Angustias viejo.

And so the circle of aqcaintances continued to expand,because whenever I was in the company of Tomás, El Marquesito and Manolito, I could be sure that by the end of the day I would have been introduced to many more of this wonderful family.

40

Other valued friendships include Dani de Utrera, a young singer who has the most ghost-like singing voice, Pocojato, non-gypsy singer with whom I have forged a special bond, Gaspar Vargas, grandson of the great El Perrate, and Jesús Requelo; son of one of Utrera's famed old singers.

It is impossible to rank your friends from a particular circle, when they all prove to be such good and respectable people, yet I must admit to having one friend in Utrera whom I consider a little more distinctive than the rest.

He is not, in fact, related to the Pinini saga, but was adopted into the bosom of their clan when he first arrived in Utrera in the early 1940s.

Manuel Requelo can only be described as the 'salt of the earth' - the kind of Gypsy who truly flourishes when in the company of his family and friends.

The dirt on which Andalusia was erected is running through this man's veins and the thrill of his timeworn cante is not perfection, but astoundingly Gypsy.

His family own a bar in the backstreets of the town and I have the fondest memories of numerous bustling orgies of flamenco, which inevitably flowed well into the night-hours. These shindigs normally start in the afternoon with a quiet lunch, digested with a glass or two of *Tio Pepe*, and then slowly it progresses into a night of unrestrained gratification.

Manuel is never so at ease as when he is surrounded by his family, especially his grandson Jesús; a boisterous two-year old that is already naturally infected with the mysteries of his people's art.

His father, Jesús de la Frasquita, is one of Utrera's most notable young flamenco singers, and Jesús junior has adapted his father's mannerism almost to perfection.

At present, his slaps and stomps are a little off balance, but one can clearly see that this seedling will flourish because of the magical sediment that flows in his blood.

One fond memory that has been tattooed in my mind happened during a weeklong celebration, throughout which, Utrera celebrated some of its greatest flamenco families.

The highlight of the proceedings was a gala show in the *Teatro Enrique de la Cuadra*, involving members of each of these regal flamenco families.

Whenever there is an event of this scale in Utrera, I inevitably cancel anything else that I should probably be doing, in favour of a few days in this delightful old town.

I had arranged to meet Luis el Marquesito beforehand at a small bar close to the theatre.

A charmingly polite person, Luis is always at the centre of the party, and his mischievous, natural born sense of humour make him the perfect host.

Tonight though, he was restless and uneasy about the show, and whilst the rest of the group exchanged conversation and cigarettes, Luis stood at the bar psyching himself in his whiskey.

I was present in order to write a review for a flamenco magazine, so I did not have to queue with the hundreds of people out front; I followed the entourage through the artiste's entrance and into the back stage area.

Whilst the musical director conversed with the maestros of the show, I decided to wander into the lobby to see who was in attendance.

The doors had not yet been opened and so the small side street was bursting with people, and the first thing I spotted was the 'salt and pepper' mane of Manuel Requelo.

Manuel had his back to the window and almost leapt in the air as I hammered on it to get his attention; the only word I could make out was the initial one -*Cabron*!

'Give me one of your menthol cigarettes', he demanded, as I stepped out into the street to greet him.

We had time, so he informed me, to have a quick drink before the doors opened, and so we slipped off to the *Bar Gomez Miguel*, which is close to the theatre.

This bar is one of the most nostalgic, and certainly one of the most interesting, pubs in Utrera, and the outside of this old tavern shows no hint of the treasures that are waiting inside.

You are transported back to the sepia era of Andalucía, because this establishment seems to have let the door shut out the twenty-first century: the smell of sweet wine oozes from old wooden barrels, the floor is awash with litter, and the walls adorned with old newspaper clippings and pictures of Utrera's legends and landmarks. The clientele look like they have just climbed down from one of the many fading photographs that are pinned haphazardly around the bar, and the appearance of an extremely tall Englishman stops most of them in full sentence.

A handful of flat-capped men were leant against the heavy wooden bar top; all of whom greeted Manuel with a respect and cordiality that he seems to receive wherever he goes. Manuel is always the first to get a juerga going and the scenes that unfolded before my eyes on this occasion were what best describe the real meaning of the flamenco way of life.

Manuel, and an ever-increasing group of people, started to clap out the rhythm of the *buleria*, which prompted one toothless old chap to burst into song. The faint tones of his cracked chords was almost lost in the clapping of hands and stamping of feet, but faces lit-up as his spontaneously invented lyrics had the impact that was intended.

Impromptu dance outbursts were met with indisputable Gypsy enthusiasm and the sheer happiness and elation that engulfed this small bar was nothing short of magical, and the spontaneity of it all, truly mesmerising.

But it was over in a matter of minutes and much to my disappointment, they all soon returned to their conversations as if nothing had occurred. I was left wondering what had instigated the outburst in the first place.

Most of my meetings in Utrera, whether planned or unscheduled, are usually connected to flamenco and, or, El Pinini, but occasionally something excellent will come out of a most unexpected encounter. I have often been treated like a visiting ambassador when I am in this town and the one thing that is foremost during any fiesta or gathering, is the Gypsy's simple lust for life, and the wanting need to share it.

Introductions invariably lead onto other avenues and my net of friends, acquaintances and colleagues with in this world, is today, much larger that I could ever have contemplated.

Nearly all of these connections have come from the families of El Pinini and El Perrate, whilst others have evolved from sessions at the *casa de cultura* and the ayuntamiento, interviews with local radio and television, fiestas during the feria, and so forth.

I spent many hours, during my research for the book concerning El Pinini, in the civil registry and at various churches in search of old documents and certificates.

The municipal library was another place where I would get lost for days on end, whilst searching through the vast selection of literature available in their archives.

My face soon became familiar to the people that work in these establishments and they all, whether priest, receptionist or deputy mayor, offered help and assistance of the highest degree.

The people of Utrera are proud of their history and eager to share it and it is this kind of openness and warmth that makes this old town so marvellous.

Bronze and dream, the gypsies came through the olive grove, their heads held high, their eyes half closed.

F. Garcia Lorca

Gypsy Ballads

There is an inexplicable sensation that races through my body whenever I see the destination illuminated on the front of the train as it rolls into the station at Dos Hermanas.

On this particular cold blustery night in February, I stood on the platform trying to calculate how many times I had made this journey during the previous eight-years. Of course, I had no idea, but thankfully, the train arrived and averted my attention from such a meaning-less task and I was soon en route to Utrera once again.

My residence in Utrera is a small boarding house in the Calle Jerusalem called the *Hostal Hidalgo1,* and this pleasant little retreat is owned by a bubbly individual by the name of Charo.

Charo is a respected friend of the family of El Perrate; many of whose children she grew up with in these very same streets.

El Perrate lived just a few yards away from the hostel, at number 22 Calle Teresa de Jesús, and it was outside this small terraced house that the singer would spend his final days, confined to a wheel chair and with little more than his wonted cigarette for enjoyment.

The home is still in the possession of his family and today his daughter Maria lives in the house that has since become something of a shrine to her late father.

Photographs highlighting the golden years of the 1970s stand on the sideboard in the tiny living room, along with trophies and possessions that were given to a man whose mastery of the Gypsy cante of this area is unequalled.

In his final years, El Perrate looked a sad shadow of the great singer he had once been, but he is a part of the backcloth that is still greatly missed by all who knew and loved him.

The people who live in this area are what city folk may call a *cateto,* which roughly translated means a villager, but it needs to be used in the correct context because it could be received as an insult.

It can also mean peasant, and so one can see how it can offend, but the word can signify rustic, and it is this connotation that I use to describe the residents of these small backstreets.

They are humble, but strong willed, down-to-earth, though plain speaking, friendly, yet cautious, and although they are simple people who want little; they are honest people who give openhandedly.

Charo is respected and admired by everyone because of her charitable nature, and it would appear that she has always gone out of her way to help those less fortunate.

She validated this munificent temperament when she once came across a family of Romanians sleeping in the doorway of a local bank.

The homeless couple possessed nothing more than two plastic sacks and two grubby-faced, undernourished urchins that were huddled on a filthy old blanket.

Distressed at their plight and saddened by the feeble state of the children, she offered the family free food and lodgings at the hostel: a few weeks later, she arranged a charity flamenco night in the grounds of her family's summer chalet, where dozens of her flamenco acquaintances performed to raise money for the family.

She also took the case to the press and after her plea on national television; the family received an offer of work and accommodation on a farm in Jaen[7]

It was because of the compassion of the people of Utrera that I found myself back in the town on a bitterly cold night during the month of February, because a huge musical extravaganza had been organized in aid of a sick child who needed desperate medical aid.

Charo works in her brother's bar when the hostel is quiet during the winter, and at this time of year I am often the only person in residence. The normal procedure is to announce my arrival at the bar and then Charo will accompany me to the hostel in order to check me in.

I arrived on this particular night at around 10pm and the tiny bar was packed and somewhat boisterous, and Charo and her brother were trying desperately to satisfy the noisy rabble. Whilst pouring a glass of beer with one hand and taking the money from the customer with the other, Charo asked if I would mind letting myself into the hostel: 'You should know

---

[7] Unfortunately, this particular family obviously had no intention of working and soon breached this agreement. They were to be given another two different opportunities, but after constant refusal to comply with the conditions they had been offered, they returned to a life on the streets.

your way around by now', she claimed; whilst letting the frothing larger flow over the glass and on to the floor.

The following day, after coffee and a late breakfast, I decided to wander over to the venue of the charity gig, which was due to start at 1pm.

The dusty road leading to the feria ground looked rather bleak and vacant, and the trees stood motionless and without ornamentation.
There were no bunting-festooned marquees or pristine horse-drawn carriages, nor the usual hubbub of the fairground; the whole place was desolate.

I made my way to the far end of the park in order to get to the municipal pavilion, where around seven-hundred people had turned out to enjoy a copious supply of paella and alcohol, and some excellent homegrown music.

53

Numerous flamencos and various blues and rock outfits gave their support in order to raise money for this sick child, and the afternoon would soon develop into a frenzy of high-wired gitanerias.

I must admit to feeling rather nostalgic whilst watching the rock outfits during their sound-checks, and it was rather amusing to see many of the characteristic old Gypsy women sitting in the front row; seemingly unperturbed by the monotonous pounding of the drums pulsating from the huge speakers.

The pavilion began to fill with dozens of familiar faces and whilst the women tussled for seats, the men headed to the bar, which is where most of them stayed for the duration of the afternoon.

Trilby hats, flat caps, white suits, gold teeth, rotting teeth, medallions, pearls, silk shawls and cashmere scarves adorned the bodies of these compatible bohemian characters.

It would have been well worth the insignificant three-euro entrance fee just to be absorbed in this atmosphere, and to observe the poetic characters that were in attendance: indeed they were an artist's impression of everything that is truly Andalusian, but it is not only the older generation to which I refer, because the younger ranks are of similar countenance.

One such individual, who swanked past like a young Rolling Stone, was Daniel Gonzalez Gutierrez, better known as Dani de Utrera.

Born in Utrera in 1980, Dani was taken under the wing of the family of El Perrate and it was they who influenced the strange flamenco style that he has since developed.

His paternal grandfather was from Las minas de Rio Tinto in Huelva, but he lived most of his life in Lebrija, and it was in the near-by town of Las Cabezas de San Juan that he had met Dani's grandmother.

He was said to have written the most wonderful poetry, but Dani knows little about his grandfather because he was a victim of the Civil war: Dani is another of the thousands of young Spaniards whose families were torn apart by this vicious conflict, and he grew up tormented by stories of the horrors that were inflicted on his ancestors.

Dani was raised in the traditional Gypsy manner of Utrera and his childhood memories are full of family fiestas where his mother would dance and his father would accompany on the guitar.

Dani had been given a guitar when he was a child, but he was more motivated by the *cante*, and he was greatly inspired by

El Perrate: he claims that this was the key that opened the lock of his profound passion of flamenco singing.

He also acknowledges that Gaspar de Utrera made a huge impact on his life, and it was a great privilege, he once told me, to have known and experienced Gaspar's massive talent.

One can hear a subliminal resonance of both El Perrate and Gaspar de Utrera in Dani's style, especially when singing the *soleá*, during which his voice shakes and vibrates with agonizing sorrowfulness.

Dani's convivial nature is always foremost, and his erratic dance explosions and earthy style of singing is a reminder of the great young talent that can be found in Utrera.

Dani's habitual accompanist is Amador Gabarri, a young guitarist who was raised in the nearby town of Dos Hermanas, or *quarto tetas*, as it is jokingly referred[8].

He began to play the guitar at the age of fourteen and quickly installed himself into the Utrera tradition, and now he regularly accompanies Tomás de Perrate; he is also establishing himself as one of the young jazz influenced soloists.

56

---

[8]Dos Hermanas means 'two sisters'; hence its nickname of 'four tits'

It is often the non-professionals that are implanted in one's memory, especially after one has encountered a spontaneous flamenco outpouring during a private get-together.

During a previous feria in Utrera, I had witnessed a young singer perform in one of the *casetas* and this performance has left me with a memorable impression, because he displayed a natural confidence that many professional performers seem to lack.

I had spotted this same young singer on the far side of the pavilion on this particular afternoon and I was delighted to learn that he was indeed to perform at the concert.

Just a few minutes later, he bounded onto the stage with an ingenuous animal-like instinct, and he possessed a natural ability to transmit the spirit of flamenco to his audience.

These are the occasions when flamenco releases it's true identity - and occasionally the *duende* - and no words can describe it, because it is a happening that evaporates as quickly as it appears, leaving one feeling breathless – speechless!

This naturalism makes the pure Gypsy flamenco prevail over anything that one may experience in the surroundings of a commercial setting.

Even though this event was organized, what took place on the stage was not, it was merely a group of gypsies doing what comes so natural to them.

This young prodigy is Juan Suarez Amaya, or El Bomba as he is affectionately known; a fourteen year old Gypsy whose family originates from *Las Tres Mil Viviendas* in Seville.

The 'Three Thousand Homes' is a notorious ghetto neighbourhood in Seville that comprises of six districts; two of which, *Murillo* and *Las Vegas,* are considered the most dangerous slums of Seville.

Many of the homes in these areas are without hot water or electricity, and the public services will often refuse to enter without a police escort.

The estate houses approximately twenty-thousand gypsies, many of whom left Triana during the 1970s, and today the area has one of the biggest problems of coexistence.

It is also an area that has the highest population of children that have never attended school and the largest amount of clan or family wars: it is also a main pool of flamenco and is rich in the production of performers.

Thankfully, El Bomba seems to have escaped the illegitimate life-style of this notorious area and has channelled his drive into flamenco, and he certainly has an exceptional understanding of his people's tradition.

One may hope that he will go on to better things and possibly follow the path to national, or even international, stardom, but one also hopes that he will never lose his effortless drive. All too often, the natural instinct that these youngsters possess is lost or destroyed in the turmoil of the commercial world.

Flamenco is simply a tradition that is passed from one generation to the next and it will be the likes of El Bomba, and there are many others like him, who will help to continue this simple Gypsy art for many years to come.

After the rousing performance of El Bomba, I headed back-stage to the artiste's area, which consisted of a small marquee tent that was marginally bigger than a dolls house.

It was a bitterly cold afternoon and so everyone was huddled inside, and as cigarettes were continuously lit, whiskey filled paper cups were given to who ever held out their hand.

Manolito de Angustias, Gaspar de Perrate, El Marquesito and Dani de Utrera were warming up with the rhythm of the bulerias; although engaging in the *palmas* was more likely to have been an excuse to warm their hands.

Gaspar is one the old school style performers who is at his best performing in this type of atmosphere and he will inevitably engage in a little of his 'grandfather' style dance.

His jacket will be hitched above his waste to reveal the back of his baggy trousers gyrating to the rhythm; an outburst that lasts just a few seconds, before he adjusts his jacket and composes himself to continue singing.

Dani de Utrera's voice was the most audible above the din, and the notes seemed to peel from the edges of his deepest emotions, as his voice vibrated around the canvas surroundings.

Dani's art is void of ornamentation and his cante is stripped to the bare bark: when singing *siguiriyas* or *soleares* his echo is intensely chilling, but when singing the fiesta styles, his powerful intonation is discharged with the force of a volcano.

The small marquee was rattling with bulerias and cantinas, and one almost forgot that there was a scheduled concert taking place on the other side of the stage.

The impromptu session came to an end when an official appeared to inform El Marquesito and the clan that it was their turn next.

As the guys disappeared through the back of the stage, I was left holding mobile phones, bunches of keys and numerous packs of cigarettes and lighters.

Even though these shows are always excellent entertainment, on this occasion, the ambience was lost, and the flamencos looked somewhat out of place between the glittering drum-kit and huge speakers that dominated this large stage: it certainly lacked the feeling and spontaneity of what I had witness just moments before.

SANCTIFICATION

Numerous writers of varying nationalities have commented on the marvels that the province of Seville has to offer and they all seemed to have agreed about the wonderful ambience that engulfs the region in times of celebration.

Many of these people had experienced Seville during the Semana Santa celebrations and from what they have described; it would appear that little has changed today during this week of spiritual mayhem.

Richard Ford was astounded by what he witnessed in 1830 and he questioned how anything ever got done in Seville, because every day appeared to be a holiday.

Andalusia's association with music and fiesta goes back hundreds of years and the necessity for joyous celebration is as hereditary as their fascination with religion and death.

Andalusia is transformed into a colourful podium during Easter week and most of the people get just as much enjoyment from the theatrical aspect of Easter, as they do from the religious side. Many have questioned the authenticity of this week of religious turbulence, and it is often dismissed as just another excuse to dress up and party. Walter Starkie, who made his living as an itinerant musician in Andalusia at the beginning of the 1920s, observed that in general, the Andalusians have a love of acting up to what foreigners expect of them.

There is though, a devotion and commitment that these people hold for their preferred image, and the belief that some of these images possess special healing powers is enough to keep them devout.

I have experienced this week of deeply religious indulgence in many different areas of Andalusia, and whilst not wanting to get into the age-old altercation concerning whose are the best, it has been in the province of Seville that I have witnessed the most memorizing scenes.

Semana Santa is celebrated differently in Andalusia compared to the rest of Spain, and all of the eight provinces are spectacular with regards to their floats and the way in which they are conveyed.

The *tronos,* as they are called in Malaga, are huge in comparison to those of Seville, but their size makes them no more impressive.

In Seville they are called *pasos,* and these floats are generally smaller in order for them to be manoeuvred around the tiny streets that surround the cathedral: one is held in awe at the skill and precision that is required in order to do this, and the emotion generated will depend on factors that most foreigners fail to perceive entirely.

The way the floats are decorated, the particular gown that the virgin is wearing, even the route that she takes, will all be of great significance. Above all else, however, the way in which the float is carried will be of most importance and this will depend greatly on the skill of the *costaleros.*

The costaleros are the pallbearers that carry the mammoth weight of the float on their shoulders, and there are certain areas in Seville where they will be forced to manoeuvre this huge mass, whilst shuffling along the narrow cobbled streets on their knees.

I will admit that I did not understand most of what I witnessed, during the Easter week in Andalusia, and at first I found the endless waiting on street corners rather tedious.

Today however, I have become a lot more aware of what is happening, and instead of simply willing away the time, I can now appreciate the emotion and stimulation that is generated during these processions.

Much of my understanding concerning Semana Santa stems from my experiences in Triana, because members of my extended Spanish family belong to the brotherhood of *La Trianera*.

One can, unfortunately, become lost and confused in the turmoil and excitement of the massive processions that take place in the centre of the city, and at times, it can become somewhat overwhelming.

Over the years, I have witnessed numerous processions in Seville, but I must admit that I found the atmosphere and the reception much more enjoyable in the small towns and villages.

The first procession in Utrera commences on Palm Sunday from the *Basilica de Maria Auxiliadora,* and this procession passes by the town hall and it is from one of the balconies of this grandeur building that the first saeta of Easter will be performed.

The saeta is a religious mantra that would normally be sung to the religious images as they are carried through the streets. This song can be performed by anyone who feels emotionally moved, although today practiced singers at organized points along the route generally sing the saeta; therefore, it loses much of its naturalness.

The most rousing experience will normally come in the early hours, when the lone voice will vibrate through the night air like death itself.

The air is fragranced with the incense that bellows from the ornate *incieniarios,* which are gently swung from a long silver chain: the sudden *cluck, cluck, cluck* of the *llamador* signals that the song is over.

The float is then lifted in a single swift movement, instigating much appreciation from the spectators, and the elaborate silver poles that support the lavish velvet canopy, swing to an eerie rhythm as the float disappears into darkness

The saeta will differ slightly from town to town and the oldest are believed to be those of Arcos de Frontera in Cadiz, although another theory cites the saeta of Alcalá de Guardaira in Seville to be even older than those of Cadiz.

The saeta from Jerez de la Frontera is called *Saeta jerezano de siguiriya*, whilst the *Saeta Malagueña* will incorporate both the siguiriya and the martinete, giving it a rather Gregorian tone.

The saeta malagueña is rather long and quite difficult to perform correctly and some singers will perform only in the style of the martinete, in order to avoid the high notes of the siguiriya.

The saeta of Utrera is based on the siguiriya and it takes a well-matured voice to perform it correctly. Antonio 'Niko' Peña and Jesús de la Frasquita are two of the best performers of them, and these two traditional singers will often perform the saeta during the procession of the gypsies.

Referred to as *Los Gitanos*, this is one of the occasions during Easter week when the spontaneity of the saeta will be unaffected.

Thursday night, and the early hours of Friday morning, is by far the most popular part of Semana Santa in Utrera.

The first procession of Maundy Thursday leaves the *Capilla de la Trinidad* at 7pm, and its itinerary will pass through the *Arco de Villa*. Much skill and competence is needed for the procession to pass through this historic archway, and yet the whole procedure is accomplished with meticulous precision.

The second parade of the night leaves the colossal church of Santiago three hours later, and this silent procession is quite an astonishing experience.

The only sound one hears is the shuffling of esparto shoes and the rattling of the *varales* as the pasos pass through the dark streets.

Varales are the silver poles that support the canopy that covers the virgin, and the costaleros will gently rock the float so that they will create a rhythmic clattering.

The most popular event of this night though, is the procession of the gypsies.

This exciting cavalcade leaves the Santiago Church at half-past midnight, and during the five-hour trajectory, the gypsies sing and dance continuously to the images of the *Cristo de la Beuna Muerte* and the *Virgin de la Esperanza*[9].

The streets along which the procession will pass are lined with thousands of people, and one of the highpoints of the

---

[9]Christ of the good death and the Virgin of hope.

night comes when the virgin is presented at the portal of the *Iglesia de San Fransico*.

This much-worshipped image of the Virgin Mary will then be manoeuvred back and forth in the entrance, but she will not enter; she is merely paying her respects as she passes the open doors of the church.

As the procession moves on along the Calle Virgen de Consolacion, an unbounded supply of flower petals is showered down onto the virgin from the roof tops of the old palatial houses that line this narrow street. The display is fervently received by the spectators, and the incessant sprinkle of floral adornment gives one the sensation of something quite mystical.

This night is celebrated in time-honoured Gypsy demeanour, and during the early hours the tiny streets of Utrera will ring with the singing of saetas, siguiriyas, bulerias and soleares.

This procession once passed along the celebrated Calle Nueva, but in recent years, the local council has decided that this is no longer practical.

It was once traditional for the saeta to be sung from the balcony of the house of Manuel de Angustias, and some of the greatest singers have sung to the images from the window of this quaint house in the Calle Nueva.

There is something quite mystical about this old street, because so many illustrious singers were born and raised there.

Obviously the street has changed since the days when El Pinini and his wife Josefa raised their nine children there, yet there are certain parts of this cobbled street that have barely changed at all.

The old house where La Fernanda and La Bernarda de Utrera were born is little more than a brick-bare shell today, but the small house where Manuel de Angustias once lived has hardly altered.

The front door leads to a small patio filled with geraniums, jasmine and numerous dangling pot-plants. The facade of the building still sports the wrought-iron balcony railings where Antonio Mairena and Manolo Caracol once stood in order to perform the saeta.

The tradition of the gypsies in Utrera stretches back five centuries and the profound mysteries of their art and culture seem to have been impregnated in the stones of these old houses where they once lived.

El Sol de los Gitano's

The assumption that many of the Easter processions will be disrupted due to torrential rain is almost a foregone conclusion, and the Semana Santa of which I now speak was to be no exception to this reckoning.

Many Andalusians had hoped that their week of religious indulgence would be spared the habitual rain that typically arrives during the weeklong celebrations, but this was not to be so in Utrera during this particular Easter.

Occasional showers interrupted the first few days, but most of the processions managed to their complete their journeys without too much interference.

The previous few weeks had seen temperatures in the high twenties, with clear, sunny skies, but come Maundy Thursday, a black thunderous haze gathered overhead like an advancing army.

The sun occasionally appeared from behind the charcoal-black clouds, and the brilliant outline of cinnamon that lit the sky was quite astounding.

This is known as *El Sol de los Gitanos* - the Gypsy's sun. This expression has many theories as to its origin, but it appears to stem from their incessant yearning for the great outdoors, and not, as has been suggested, because of black legend or sorcery.

Indeed, it rained torrentially on this day and the sun never materialized at all, but the skies eventually cleared around 9pm and a ray of hope smothered the thousands of expectant people that were jammed in to the Plaza Altozano.

Many of the women were dressed in black and crowned with ornamental hair combs and trailing lace *mantillas.* During the daytime, it is traditional to wear a much smaller *peineta*, but at night, the grandest and most decorative combs are sported.

The austere attire is complemented with silk or lace gloves, strings of pearls and broaches of precious stones; a demonstration of the stateliness these people display at Easter.

Even more people began to converge on the plaza, as it seemed that the rain might well have ceased for the night.

Dozens of excited children ran screeching like a flight of chirping swallows, whilst parents and grandparents surveyed the sky in anticipation of a full moon.

My attention was diverted to the huge wingspan of a Stork that was circling above us. These wonderful creatures are a regular sight in Utrera and this particular one resides on the bell tower of the *Iglesia de San Francisco.*

The accustomed atmosphere of Utrera was replaced with the hullabaloo of the town's folk, who were spilling out of the bars and cafes; all hopeful that *El Cautivo* would embark on his silent procession.

This procession, known as *El Silencio,* has no musical accompaniment and many of the black-robed *nazarenos* will endure great pain during the five hour journey, because they are bare footed and shackled at the ankles. The sound of the chains scraping along the cobbles is somewhat eerie and the flickering candles and cross-bearing, hooded penitents offer the whole scene a rather medieval ambience.

By the time I arrived at the church on this night, most of the nazarenos and costaleros were looking rather dismayed by the probability that, once again, their hopes would be shattered by mother-nature.

There was a feeling that the rain was not in fact over, so the brotherhood had announced that *El Cautivo* would not be leaving the church. The decision was soon endorsed when the heavens opened once again.

There was still almost three hours before the procession of the Gypsies was to commence, and all prayers were beseeching for an intermission of the appalling weather.

The sky had cleared again by midnight and the nazarenos began to arrive in droves; their long white robes shimmering in the moonlight as they disappeared through the small side entrance known as the *puerta de sacristia*.

One young Gypsy began to sing, and he sang to god to thank him for the stars that he had bequeathed them, and for the moon that would guide them on their journey, but his hopes quickly diminished as word spread that the brotherhood were about to hold a meeting to decide if the procession was to go ahead.

Various bigwigs of the brotherhood hurried through the side entrance, politely ignoring the pleas of the waiting crowds.

The main doors of the church remained closed at this stage because access is restricted and, unless you are connected or invited, there is little chance of gaining entry. Even the local television company were refused admission by the extremely authority-provoked attendant, although they eventually gained entry with the assistance of one of the hierarchy of the brotherhood.

But soon the crashing of the thunderous clouds and another heavy downpour virtually confirmed our worst fears, so I decided to go in search of someone who may be able to smuggle me inside. My prayers were answered faster than I had expected, when an immaculately dressed Manuel Requelo appeared from the small side door, puffing on what was obviously a much-needed cigarette.

He assured me that he would indeed accompany me inside the church, after, of course, he had inhaled sufficient nicotine.

After extinguishing the cigarette under the sole of his shoe, he ushered me through the small side entrance, whilst informing the watchful attendant that I was his guest.

One would have been forgiven for overlooking the fact that this is a consecrated place of worship, because the ambience inside the church was elevating.

The scenes were reminiscent of a scriptural film-set because of the diversity of the differing vestments.

Boys dressed in lace and gold-trimmed velvet gowns stood around the church in clusters, their decorative silver candleholders held high above their heads like the spears of centurions.

The black and white chequered marble floor of the church seemed to merge with the long white robes of the nazarenos and harmonize with their black pointed hoods.

Costaleros were helping each other to secure their turban-like head wear, whilst others assisted with the corsets that are worn in order to give support when they are carrying the colossal weight of the float.

Some wore fleece jackets with the shield of the fellowship embroidered on the front, and the words 'Gitano', in gold, on the back.

Two laurel branches that encircle an anchor, which is topped with a crown of thorns, form the shield: the anchor is a symbol of hope, whilst the cross at the top of the anchor signifies Christ's death.

The sound of brass could be heard over the hum, as eager musicians toyed with their instruments, and silk-gowned youths swung ornate silver casks from long chains, filling the church with musky incense.

A nervous tension was generated by the important, and rather anxious, looking members of the brotherhood, as they rushed about trying to secure a decision.

The congregation was eventually hushed - well almost - because the head of the *cofriada* was clearing his throat in order to give a short speech to tell of the inevitable.

Heads fell to the floor as the flock was informed that the rehearsals and hard graft had not been in vain, but as the praise and acknowledgments continued, many were too overcome to listen. People were hugging, and reassuring each other, whilst others sat in the wings wiping occasional tears that ran down their sad faces.

Yet it was not long before the ambience and volume augmented once again; especially when the marching band started up inside the church.

The brass echoed around the high Baroque arches of the Santiago church like the wrath of the gods: as one band stopped, another struck up, and the music at least put some joy back into the faces of the congregation.

Once the bands ceased, the singing started, and yet the clapping hands and broken voices were hardly audible above the commotion of the church.

It was a sad time for the people of Utrera, because they would have to wait another year before they could celebrate the night of the gypsies in the established manner.

A VERY GOOD FRIDAY

Good Friday arrived and it was obvious that the rain was here to stay for the foreseeable future, and the flooded streets of Utrera stood gloomy and empty.

The majestic red velvet balcony covers that normally hang with regal dignity during Easter were now sopping wet and wilting, and the wooden seats remained stacked in their piles at the side of the road.

The first procession of Good Friday would normally leave the *Capilla de San Bartolmé* at 7 am, but it was cancelled because of the enduring rain.

The second procession, *Santo Entierro,* was scheduled to leave the *Iglesia de San Francisco* at 7pm.

The *Hermandad y cofradia de la Santa Vera Cruz* was founded in 1280 and it is the oldest in Utrera, but, as had been expected, there had been no choice but to cancel yet another of the final processions of the week.

There was however, one celebration planned for the day that the rain would not postpone, and this was a party that was to take place in one of Utrera's emblematic old bars.

The bar is just a short walk from the main plaza, but on this atrocious afternoon, a taxi was necessary due to the monsoon that was sweeping through the town.

The roads turned into raging rivers and the sheer volume of water created scenes similar to the December of 1962 when the river Calzas Anchas burst its banks[10].

It was around three o clock when I arrived, and I sank ankle deep in rainwater as I leapt out of the taxi. The bar was relatively empty, although the Requelo family were in the middle of a huge lunch that was spread across three or four wooden tables. Manuel rearranged the chairs and instructed his daughter to organize a plate of *puchero;* he then filled a glass with a dark, pungent, matured sherry.

Puchero is one of Andalusia's most staple dishes and it is a hearty meal perfect for heating and nourishing the body in times of extreme weather. Made with chicken, pork, chorizo,

---

[10]The great flood of 1962 destroyed the patio, kitchen and library of the Salisiano School and also did considerable damage to areas like El Niño Perdido.

chick-peas, potatoes, vegetables and rice, this wholesome soup is eaten as a two course meal: first the soup of chick-peas, rice and vegetables, followed by the meat – *pringa,* which is mashed together with the potatoes and plenty of olive oil.

This soup is cooked with an array of bones, pork fat and bacon, and the aroma and flavour is truly rustic, but there are secrets to achieving a truly authentic dish[11].

The addition of a glass of fino, or sherry, at the end of its cooking time is considered essential; especially if one is nursing a hangover.

Once the food was over, and the plates removed, it was time to relax, and as cigarettes were lit and glasses re-filled, the conversation again turned to the washout Easter.

As is usual, Manuel acted as coordinator and soon had us all sitting in a semi-circle, and within seconds, the rhythm of the buleria was supported by all present.

Our attention was momentarily directed to a small guy who had pulled his chair into the centre, in order to dance the buleria whilst seated.

---

[11]It is deemed necessary to use a cock – *gallo,* and not a hen -*pollo,* in order to get a truly authentic tasting puchero.

At first, his head was bowed and his hands clasped as if in prayer, then, in a similar manner to the late Farruco, whom he strangely resembled, his head suddenly rose, and slowly, he began to move.

His body began to contort and his face drooped almost stroke-like, as he warped his distorted body around the structure of the rhythm.

His facial movements were somewhat hideous, but it was the movement of his elongated features that performed the best dance.

We were all elevated and stimulated by this man's art, and the enjoyment he instigated in those few moments were most certainly one of the highpoints of this Easter week.

Whilst we were enjoying the impromptu juerga, I had failed to notice that the bar was quickly filling, and many of the most renowned flamencos of the town were now in attendance.

One of the wonderful things about these types of gatherings is the incredible family togetherness, because just about everyone in the room is related.

The afternoon's flamenco was being supplied by Jesús de la Frasquita, Mari Peña, and Joselito de la Buena; a short, tanned Gypsy who sings in a manner that is seldom heard today.

The bar was packed and noisy and Joselito could barely be heard above the din, but eventually, and after much shushing, we were able to appreciate his timeworn quality.

Now in his seventies, Joselito is one of the old-school singers whose voice has that bronzed maturity, and even the powerful voice of Jesús de la Frasquita lacked this hard-earned quality.

One characteristic old Gypsy took to the floor to dance, and as he clapped and cheered himself along, a sprightly grandmother joined in with some amusing, and rather provocative, movements. They were soon engaged in a hilarious dance routine that had everyone howling, and they strutted and stomped until they could barely breathe.

The locals joined in with encouraging *jaleo* from various corners of the room, and excited faces peered through the window from the street outside, because there was simply no space in the bar.

During the *fin de fiesta,* and after a considerable amount of Tio Pepe, Manuel Requelo, and several others in our group, began badgering me to dance.

Before I had the time to resist, I was shoved into the middle of the proceedings and had no option but to do something, however hideous it might have looked.

Somewhat reluctantly, I bent my knees and scrunched the bottom of my jacket with my left hand, and then blundered across the floor, whilst twirling my right hand, like a demented fool.

This outburst caused much excitement among the children, who shrieked with excitement; *'Mira, mira; el inglés alto intenta bailar por buleria!*

However, my performance lasted just a few seconds, after which, I dashed back to the bar, and out of the sight of the excited ragamuffin kids.

Manuel, who had to remove his glasses in order to wipe away the tears of laughter, assured me that I had at least saved face by participating.

My only consolation was that my bumbling routine was over as quickly as it had begun, and so no one had time to reach for their cameras.

After much teasing and light repartee at my expense, I decided that it was probably time to make my exit; for if I had been so drunk as to dance, I was surely too drunk to continue!

I awoke around eight-thirty the following morning and I decided to walk to the centre to clear my head and find some much-needed caffeine.

The streets were quiet except for a few women who were busily mopping, or sweeping, their front porches, and the odd beggar who would mumble at a volume barely audible, whilst holding an out-stretched arm in anticipation of a few coins.

The tyres of the cars will normally screech at this time of year, due to the wax that drips onto the roads from the tapers and candles of the nazarenos, but this year little wax had fallen and the cars passed in relative silence.

The tranquillity of the morning was interrupted by the sudden rattling and banging of a trolley that was piled high with household rubbish and things of little value.

Clinging nervously to the handles of the uncontrollable cart was a stout Gypsy woman who had the glare of a wolf in search of prey.

I watched as she rummaged a few open top bins in hope of some reward, but it would appear that there was little of any good to be had.

I eventually arrived at the bar *El Pollo*, which, thankfully, was free of anyone other than the barman.

This small bar is just a short walk from the *Mercado de Abastos,* and here they serve toasted flat bread-rolls called *molletes*, and coffee that is so fragrant, the aroma alone will alert even the most tired mind.

The sun was shining and, although black clouds hung in the distance, it appeared that the rain might at last be over; sadly, so was the best part of Easter.

LEBRIJA AND BACK

A few days after I had returned to Málaga, following the washout Easter week in Utrera, I received an invitation to attend the first communion of Esperanza Nuñéz– the eldest daughter of Luis El Marquesito.

The celebration was to be held on the first Saturday of May and so I was soon preparing to return to the town I so unrestrainedly cherish.

The service began at midday, but I had decided to catch the train that would get me to Utrera by ten-fifteen.

I would then have time to take breakfast in the bar El Pollo and compose myself, before engaging in an afternoon of unbridled festivities with the Pinini family.

******

I arrived at Dos Hermanas train station with only seconds to spare and I just managed to leap through the bleeping doors as they were closing.

The moment the train pulled away from the station, I had a horrible gut feeling that all was not well, and how right I was to feel this way.

The electronic screen was displaying Lebrija as the next stop, and as we rattled out of the station, I soon realized that we would not be stopping in Utrera: I had actually boarded the intercity train to Cadiz, and not the circle-line to Utrera.

I quickly found the ticket vendor and explained my predicament: all I had to do, he informed me, was to change at Lebrija, which was just thirty-five minutes down the line.

I arrived in Lebrija at ten-forty, and so I assumed that I would make it back to Utrera in time for my midday rendezvous without much aggravation, and so I headed straight to the ticket office.

After studying her timetable for some considerable time, the vendor, whose voice was distortedly metallic through the perforated glass window, informed me that the next departure to Dos Hermanas was not until twelve-thirty.

It was a Saturday, hence the service was less frequent than it is during the weekdays, and I would need to return to Dos Hermanas and then take the circle line back to Utrera.

Bitterly annoyed at my stupidity, I paused to way up the situation and the options that were available at this moment in time. Unless I was prepared to pay around eighty-Euros for a taxi, which I was not, I had little chance of arriving in Utrera before half-past one.

It was obvious that I would now miss the church service and so I resigned myself to the fact that I would have to wait until the next train came along.

The train station in Lebrija is a good hike from the centre of town, but I had two hours to kill, and the thought of spending this time in a dreary train station soon had me heading in the direction of the main plaza.

I decided to seek some much needed coffee, and afterwards, seeing as I had plenty of time on my hands, I decided to stroll around the *Santa Maria de Olivia* church.

The church dominates the Plaza Rector Merina, which is the oldest and prettiest part of the town, and it was in these dusty old streets that El Pinini had once played as a child.

Built during the reign of Alfonso X in the second half of the XIII century, this outstanding church has undergone numerous major renovations, and parts of the old *Almohad* mosque that once stood on this site are still identifiable today.

The exquisite Moorish character is evident in the picturesque cloister that is enclosed with arched marble columns and perfumed with the intense aroma of jasmine and orange blossom.

The bell tower looks as though it has survived since Muslim rule, but it was actually built during 1756-1778, and the Giralda in Seville inspired this *Mudéjar* style minaret[12].

The interior of the church has a musty aroma of incense and wax, which seems to seep from its walls and the hefty, stone baptismal font looks somewhat Stone Age in comparison to the awe-inspiring decoration that invades the eye.

---

[12] It is for this reason that the bell tower of the Santa Maria de la Oliva church is affectionately known as '*Giraldilla*'

The gothic horseshoe arches and centre dome are of great architectural beauty and the superb high altar is notable for its life-like sculptures and baroque carvings.

The altar houses the shrine of the Virgin of the Olive, above which, the bruised and battered body of the crucified Christ stares down in its entire spine-chilling reality.

These magnificent effigies are the work of Alonso Cano, the great baroque artiste who earned the pseudonym of the 'Spanish Michelangelo'.

Cano's personal life however, gave rise to much malevolent gossip: his second wife, who was only twelve when they married, was brutally murdered and suspicion consequently fell on the artiste. Cano's innocence was only accepted after he had undergone considerable castigation and he eventually returned to his birthplace of Granada, where he worked on the city's cathedral until his death in 1667[13].

I left the church with my head full of extravagant religious imagery, and returned to the dazzling daylight of the painfully quiet square.

---

[13] Alonso Cano became ordained priest of the cathedral, despite disapproval from the ecclesiastical authorities, and after his death in 1667 he was interred in the cathedrals crypt.

Piled in one corner of the square, the old Pinini home resembles something from a forgotten era, yet it is still used by his descendants.

It was once the home of El Pinini's daughter, Fernanda La Vieja, and it was here that Pinini spent his final years.

El Pinini had lived almost his entire life in Utrera, but after the death of his wife, he returned to live with his daughter in Lebrija and it was in this house that he passed away.

Today the old interior patio stands derelict and rubbish strewn and certain areas of the house have been demolished, or have simply crumbled to the floor.

The small inset windows are flaking behind rusty grilles, and lopsided, black-with-mould, walls appear to be held together by the weeds that squeeze through cracks and crevices.

Electric cables dangle from rotting wooden beams like the lifeless branches of a dead vine, and the corrugated iron roof, which covers parts of the patio, is overgrown with sprouting tufts of straw-like grass.

It was once the scene of numerous flamenco parties and the dilapidated old walls would have once echoed with the singing of the Pinini clan.

The only voices heard there today are those of two scrawny looking greyhounds that bark continuously, but one can feel an uncanny presence that seems to seep from the rotting shell of this old house.

On route back to the centre of town, I saw a lone bus stop that I had failed to notice previously, and so I crossed the road and went to inspect the timetable.

The streets were deserted, except for one old guy who was leaning heavily on a walking stick, whilst puffing on the stubby-end of a cigar.
He watched with curiosity as I approached, but my attempts to converse with him were in vain. He looked at me as if I had just fallen from the sky, before muttering something unintelligible. He then spat a slither of tobacco onto the floor and waddled away as if he had not seen me in the first place.

I still had forty-five minutes before my train was due, and there was obviously no bus scheduled, so I decided to take breakfast in an old bar en-route to the station.

The dimly lit tavern had the aroma of cured meats, which was procured by the huge Serrano legs, strings of black pudding and chorizo sausages that dripped their fragrant oils onto carefully placed plates.

The noise of the coffee grinder battled with the racket coming from the television, and the sprightly barmen further destroyed any chance of a quiet breakfast as he went about his duties. The clattering of cups and saucers seemed to continue incessantly and the squealing of milk being frothed in a metal jug infiltrated my, already, aching, head.

The train rolled into Lebrija station a few minutes late and I began to panic for fear of missing my connecting train in Dos Hermanas: we arrived with barely a minute to spare and so I dashed frantically to the ticket office in order to purchase my ticket.

I already had the correct amount of change ready because I believed that the train was due any second.

The lad behind the counter obviously sensed my eagerness to grab the ticket from his hand before it had left the machine, so, reassuringly, he told me to relax: the next train to Utrera, said he, was not in fact until three-thirty![14]

I had switched off half way through his explanation and found myself wandering out into the street barely able to contain my anger.

---

[14] I had failed to notice that the times with asterisks next to them applied to weekdays only. From Monday to Friday the service runs approximately every thirty minutes, but during the weekend the service is far less frequent.

I now had only one option, and so I headed straight to the row of taxis that were waiting opposite the station: I had to pay thirty-five Euros for the privilege of listening to the driver harp-on about the new speed restrictions that had recently come into force in Spain.

The taxi eventually pulled up at the entrance to the feria ground and I exhaled a huge sigh of relief, for I was starting to believe that I would never actually arrive in Utrera at all.

El Marquesito had previously informed me that the fiesta was to be held in an old tavern that was a short walk from the *Caseta Mantoncillo*.

His directions were of little use, because nearly all of the casetas are dismantled out of feria season, and so I traipsed around the dusty open space where the feria is annually housed, in hope of stumbling upon the fiesta.

After wandering around in circles for a further twenty minutes, and whilst beginning to feel rather frustrated, I saw in the distance a young girl who was trying to attract my attention.

It was Inés, the youngest daughter of El Marquesito, and she dashed off inside to inform her father that *El Inglés* had finally arrived.

I was immediately confronted with the smiling, friendly face of El Marquesito, who greeted me with the Mediterranean hug, as opposed to the frightfully English handshake.

After I had apologized for not attending the church ceremony, and had offered my explanation why, he led me to the bar; after such an escapade, I must surely be in need of a drink, he asserted.

The venue for the communion party was a large old tavern that sits opposite the new, and extremely modern looking, bullring at the top-end of the feria ground.

Bunting, balloons and paper lanterns hung from the brick bare ceiling, and rows of wooden trestle tables were bedecked with varying plates of finger food, wine and an assortment of bottled soft drinks.

Whenever I am in the company of El Marquesito it is inevitable that the conversation will turn to his family's history and - especially during this period in time - the book that I had been working on concerning them.

Today, however, would surely be different seeing as it was his daughter's communion?

On the contrary, no sooner had I been presented with a frosted glass of beer, I was pulled to one side and asked if the book concerning his great-grandfather was nearing completion.

I offered that today was probably not a good time to discuss such things, but he assured me that we did indeed have time because the majority of the guests had not yet arrived.

The communion ceremony had been held in the small chapel in the *Salisiano School* and so there was no room for the entire family to attend the service: the people who were present at the time were the immediate family of his wife Esperanza, and some of El Marquesito's relatives that I was not familiar with.

There were two communions being celebrated that afternoon; the other was for one of El Marquesito's nephews. This chirpy nine-year old, who is known as Caracoles, wore a white military style suit braided with gold, whilst Esperanza wore a floral garland on her hair and a beautiful lace and silk gown. Together they were a picture of nobility.

El Marquesito's youngest son, Luis junior, certainly has his father's countenance, and the fact that he is little over three-years of age makes no difference to his adult-like exterior.

It wasn't long before the youngster was encouraged to demonstrate his ability to dance, and he immediately began to perform in a way that is painfully innate to these children.

As his grandfather spurred him along with outburst of song and rhythm, the tiny lad performed without coyness, but with elegance and self-possession.

His tiny arms and nimble hands twirled with the gracefulness of a swan and he moved with the distinct charisma so associated with the Pininis.

There was something quite magical in the way that Luis junior held his head and body, and one could not fail to notice the characteristic stance that his paternal grandparents once displayed.

After the first juerga of the afternoon, we returned to the bar and El Marquesito produced a plastic bottle that contained an excellent *Manzanilla* wine from the near-by town of Los Palacios, and we were soon raising our glasses and saluting the day.

El Marquesito seemed proud of the fact I had attended his daughter's communion and I was introduced to a continuing flow of his family: he probably did not realise how honoured I felt to be invited to such an intimate family event.

Numerous descendants of the infamous Pinini, one of whom was a humorous Gypsy named Fernando surrounded me.

Fernando is virtually toothless, has one lazy eye that veers to the left, and thinning grey hair that hangs in spindly strands.

He was keen to hear what I had to say about his family, but he made no bones of the fact that, because I was not of Andalusian Gypsy origin, he doubted I could have a proper understanding of their culture.

Fernando possessed that most Andalusian of characteristics that forces them, when they are convinced they are right about something, whether accurate or not, to repeat themselves continually as if to endorse what they are saying is correct.

Fernando was most definitely a member of the Pinini clan, yet he knew little about his genealogical background, although he was anxious to prove he knew more about it than me. He listened with curious expression, and interrupted on many occasions, but he seemed more intent on finding fault with my reckonings.

Eventually, and after consuming plentiful sherry, he began to demonstrate his own singing capabilities, by reciting one of Pinini's cantinas, and his conceptive expression was obviously intended to suggest that I had, indeed, witnessed the most authentic version of El Pinini's legacy.

The guests began arriving in droves and the first familiar faces I spotted were those of Manuel and Mercedes Requelo.

We were next joined by Gaspar, the grandson of the legendary El Perrate, who greeted everyone with the graciousness that appears to be inbred in this family.

Gaspar is another person who had supplied me with a stream of information concerning his family's genealogical line, and we were soon awash in conversation concerning the antics of certain members of this huge flamenco clan.

Again, the conversation turned to the massive genealogical tree that exists in Utrera and I had trouble keeping up with Gaspar, as he excitedly explained his branch of this mammoth clan.

By now, he was firing on all cylinders and his voice seemed to float off in the distance as I tried to mentally note what he was saying.

Manuel suggested that Gaspar should sing a little, and as the clapping commenced, so he began warbling in his grandfather's manner.

The short burst of inherent joviality went on practically unnoticed by the other guests, but Manuel's face lit up, his eyes suggesting surprise, and then acknowledgment, as parts of Gaspar's singing obviously touched a nerve.

Two or three other people who slotted into place to assist with the rhythm joined us, and soon Manuel's hollow voice was doing battle with the hullaballoo of the two-hundred noisy guests.

Faces illuminated as the muffled claps of the soleá intervened, followed by the trotting rhythm of the bulerias, when Manuel let rip with all he had left.

This style of flamenco contains a naturalness that flows in the blood, and because of the unadorned way in which it is performed, it is obvious that they engage in it simply for their own enjoyment.

The party was now in full swing and the neatly laid out tables were being rearranged to accommodate numerous large gatherings of people.

The click-clap-clicking of handclapping evaded the room from all corners, as numerous intimate gatherings engaged in their own separate juergas.

Another started on the far side of the room and as knuckles rapped on the tabletops, the gaily-clad women took turns at performing their fiery dance routines.

The host was kept busy greeting the never-ending flow of family and friends who continued to arrive in hordes.

The floor was littered with cigarette butts, and the tables and bar-top awash with empty glasses and bottles; and still the people were arriving.

These kind of get-togethers will normally continue until the early hours of the morning, and these revellers seemed to have an unlimited resilience and certainly seemed in no hurry to retire early.

I however, was beginning to fade, and so I embarked on the ritual tour of the room in order to say goodbye, which can, and often does, take another half hour to complete.

There is always 'one last drink' and this, no matter how resistent you are, will often be followed by yet another.

Of course, it is quite often the case that I don't really want to leave in the first place, but on this occasion my consumption maxima had been far exceeded, so I reluctantly left the fiesta and slid off into the emptiness of the night.

FIESTA

During spring and early summer, the southern-most part of Andalusia transforms into a kaleidoscope of colour and illumination, and any 'normal' routine is constantly interrupted by local celebrations, and fiestas held in recognition of more saints than most of us realize exist.

It is also the season of the time-honoured flamenco festivals that are staged in most towns and villages, and it is at these festivals that one will occasionally witlessness a little of that something that make this art so special.

Unfortunately, many of these festivals have transformed into two and three day events, and in doing so, they have lost much of the nostalgic festival ambience.

El Potaje Gitano festival in Utrera has adhered to the more orthodox style event and this coveted gathering is still organized and executed in a similar manner to when it first started back in 1957.

I have attended this popular jamboree many times and although it is always a most wonderful experience, there was one year when everyone had an extra special reason for celebration.

It was around 4pm when I stepped from the comfort of an air-conditioned carriage and into forty degrees of asphyxiating heat.

The temperature was even more intense outside and the streets were deserted, but the serenity of it all was soon invaded by the sudden buzzing of the cigarras.

The song of these seemingly invisible insects seems to be generated by the heat, because the hotter it becomes, the louder and longer they continue.

Utrera comes to life in the late afternoon and today there was excitement in the air, but it had little to do with the town's flamenco festival.

Spain had made it through to the quarterfinals of the 19th FIFA world cup, and in just a few hours, they were going to battle with the mighty Paraguay.

The main square was decorated with flags and bunting, and groups of youngsters clad in Spain's national colours gathered in the streets to sing and chant. Some had their faces painted, some wore coloured wigs, or huge floppy hats like those worn on St Patrick's Day, and a few had even dressed their dogs with red and yellow scarves. The whole town had the character of carnival.

I headed to the bar *Doña Juana*, which was crammed to the rafters, but I managed to squeeze my way through the mass of clammy bodies and jam myself wedge-like at the bar.

All eyes were glued to the television, including those of the bar staff; who would abandon whatever they were doing when things got exciting on the pitch.

The second half of the match had been in play for around twenty minutes, yet there were still no goals, so I decided to wander nearer to the Salisiano School, since the festival was soon to start.

The gates were still locked shut when I arrived at the school and, other than a handful of people milling by the road side, the scene was rather desolate.

A security guard eventually appeared from a small hut-like box and, obviously anxious to get back to his small portable television, politely informed me that the festival would not commence until after the football had finished.

Festivals of any sort rarely start on time in Andalusia and I supposed that tonight's delay had due cause.

There was a large pub on the other side of the road that was packed with anxious supporters; many of whom were stood on tiptoe in order to see the action unfold on the large television screen that was hanging from the ceiling.

As extra time seemed inevitable, the atmosphere became intense, as did the smell of alcohol and sweat, but then a sudden surge of anticipation sent people rushing towards the television.

It was as if the bar had been freeze-framed, because the din dropped instantly and mouths stretched open on panic-stricken faces. Some covered their faces or buried their heads in each other's arms; others froze with clenched fists, or simply turned their backs to the screen.

The mood was tense and jumpy, as the Spanish team fought frantically in the penalty area, but the muted encouragement rapidly elevated, as the ear splitting shrieking and yelling recommenced.

The place erupted with the force of an explosion, because David Villa had scored with just a few minutes left to play, and it looked as though Spain's prayers had finally been answered.

People flowed into the streets, their elation uncontainable and their happiness uncontrollable.

Youths hung from car windows with Spanish flags aloft; whilst others sprayed bystanders with beer and champagne, and hooters, whistles and air horns were unleashed in a continuous fanfare.

I wondered, with considerable amusement, what would happen if Spain actually made it to, and triumphed in, the world cup final![15]

I do not claim to possess a great interest in football, but I had obviously been rooting for Spain throughout the world cup. In any case, the outcome of tonight's performance would have a positive effect on the ambience of the flamenco festival. If they won, which they did, Spain's triumph would surely make the night even more wonderful than normal.

112

The *Potaje Gitano* was the first ever flamenco festival to be staged in Spain and it was organized by the brotherhood of the gypsies of Utrera. They arranged a small get-together in a makeshift marquee and one of the members of the brotherhood cooked and served a humble stew to the

---

[15] Spain went on to win the World Cup of 2010: during the final they defeated the Netherlands 1-0

relatively small audience; hence the 'Gypsy stew festival' was born.

This tradition has since been continued and still today each table is presented with a huge earthenware casserole containing the flavoursome stew; as well as two bottles of red wine that are ornamented with personal 'potaje gitano' labels.

You are also handed a small wooden spoon on entry to the festival, supposedly with which to eat the stew, but thankfully, they also supply a more conventional plastic spoon to devour this hearty feast.

The festival is held in the grounds of the Salisiano School and large round tables covered with linen cloths are spaced out across the schoolyard.

I will inevitably arrange to meet with numerous people during this festival and the first hour is always spent strolling from table to table in order to catch-up with friends and associates.

I soon came across the Requelo clan who were busily rearranging tables and chairs in order to accommodate far more people than there was available space.

Most of the gypsies bring cooler boxes laden with food and beverages and this is offered to any friends that stop by.

It is true that many of these people are not blessed with an overabundance of money, but during any of the numerous festivals that bring everyone together in the town, they will demonstrate open-handedness to an absolute extreme.

One of my fondest memories of this coveted festival was the night I first met the legendary Miguel El Funi.

Miguel is probably the closest one can get to the genuine aura of El Pinini, because he is one of the last remaining original strands of the basket.

Miguel was sporting the famous white silk scarf that has become symbolic throughout his sixty-year career, and although he is one of the oldest surviving members of the clan, he has the grace and personality of youth.

Now in the senior stages of his life, El Funi performs the kind of flamenco that one rarely witnesses today, and it is this traditional family style that is so prevailing here in Utrera.

His voice is now old and broken, but he still has that wonderful duende evoking tone that makes one's stomach ache.

I have seen many of the greatest artistes perform at this festival and even though a good few of these people have performed on some of the most diverse stages of the world; it is inevitably the descendants of El Pinini that have left me with the most treasured memories.

Each year the festival is dedicated to the honour of an individual flamenco performer or bullfighter, and occasionally someone who is simply deemed worthy of honouring.

This festival had been dedicated to the memory La Fernanda and La Bernarda de Utrera.

The festival had already honoured these celebrated sisters in 1968 and again 1997, but the third memoriam was prompted by the death of La Bernarda, who had died at the age of eighty-two the previous October.

La Fernanda and La Bernarda de Utrera were two of flamencos most illustrious singers, and on this occasion their virtuosity and talent was duly honoured from the outset.

Every opportunity to congratulate Spain's national football team was also seized, and the salutations brought roars of jubilation every time it was acknowledged.

The Potaje is renowned for the 'fiesta' that is habitually performed by members of the Pinini family, and the stage was soon awash with numerous members of this massive clan,

An ageing, and extremely frail looking, Matilde Coral, joined Luis el Marquesito, El Pitin, Luis and La Inés de Utrera, José de la Buena, Dani de Utrera and Jesús de la Frasquita.

Matilde Coral was coaxed into the fore during the fin de fiesta and the stage suddenly glowed with an almost imaginary presence.

Matilde has a radiance which fills the whole stage when she dances: her hand and arm movements are fluid and the arching of the shoulders and back done so majestically - such a contrast to the swirling hysteria performed by many of today's female flamenco dancers.

116 She is a protagonist of the 'Seville school' and this style of dance is instantly recognizable by the positioning of the dancers head, the movement of the hips and the arching of the shoulders.

Although she had to be helped onto the stage and steadied by the arm of one of the brotherhood, she instantly ignited a little of that mysterious sparkle that lays dormant until awakened by the seducing rhythm.

For sure, we were witnessing a little piece of history and one knows that this kind of happening will never be experienced again.

It was nearly five in the morning before the dancing stopped and the music faded, yet the ambience was so joyfully relaxed and the bar area was still busily engaged.

I was quickly reminded of Spain's earlier victory as I left the tranquillity of the darkened schoolyard, because the sporadic honking of horns could still be heard, and the celebrations were obviously far from over.

EXUBERANT DEVOTION

The Feria: a frenzy of gaiety, noise and colour, an onslaught of fried fish, *Tio Pepe* and dancing, and a time for celebrations that has little occasion for sleep.

The feria is one of the most enjoyable events on the Andalusian calendar and it is an event that takes place in just about every municipality.

Like most traditional aspects of this country, the feria differs from town to town, and yet the main objective that they all hold fast is to relax and enjoy a few days away from the strains every-day of life.

Málaga enjoys a grand week of celebration in August and this feria claims to be the biggest fair in Europe: it is certainly one of the most extravagant.

During the early afternoon, the maze of tiny streets that wind off the Calle Larios and Calle Granada are chockfull with thousands of revellers, and the ambience is stimulating.

One of my favorite aspects of the daytime feria in Málaga is the presence of the *Panda de Verdiales*. To the British they may resemble the infamous Morris dancers of the English countryside fetes, but, although one might find similarities in their appearance, the music is quite a different matter.

A frenzy of gaiety and color it most certainly is, and the haunting music of the violin, accompanied by the sadly Islamic tone of the singer, makes my body tingle with hurting pleasure.

The famous *'feria de abril'* in Seville is restricted to the fairground in the area of Los Remedios, and this non-stop celebration is one of the most colourful and exhilarating events in Spain.

There is, of course, an on-going altercation between the two cities as to whose feria is the grandest; although I must admit that this would be impossible to determine.

120 I have enjoyed many a jubilant afternoon during each of these sumptuous gatherings, but it is, without doubt, the intimacy of the small village ferias that I enjoy the most of all.

The feria of Utrera is another facet of the town that has not changed with the times, and even though I have attended this feria on numerous occasions, I have never come away feeling disappointed. In fact, some of my most wonderful occasions in Utrera have occurred during this period of gratifying festivity.

This feria is held on the outskirt of the town close to the bullring, and during the afternoon the casetas will be packed full of *utreranos* who dance and frolic to the razzmatazz music of the local *sevillana* groups: these groups have all the flare and tack of the old fashioned English holiday-camp bands of the nineteen-seventies.

It is a time for eating with family and friends, and it is a time to unwind and enjoy the simple pleasures of life.

Every available space is occupied by dancing couples, whose gracious movements and elegant curving come together like the perfect sculpture.

Cordovan hats and tight pinstriped pants with cummerbunds is the attire of most men, whilst the women are elegantly arrayed in a multitude of traditional designs.

Children are dressed like miniature replicas of their parents and there is a kind of exquisiteness in it all that can only be found here in the lower regions of Andalusia.

Fabulous pristine carriages parade around the dusty streets of the feria, and the fine horses that run these distinguished coaches are groomed and dressed as elegantly as the beautiful specimens that sit atop them.

The Andalusian horse evolved from the Iberian Peninsula, where its ancestors have roamed for thousands of years, and its conformation has changed little over the centuries.

The movement of the horse is cadenced and harmonious and it is renowned for its prowess, intelligence and its affection for humans. When treated with respect they are quick to learn and extremely responsive, and it has been used as a sign of nobility since the fifteenth-century; thus earning it the designation of 'Horse of kings'.

The Andalusian horse is very noble and gracious, and their regimental-like obedience is a sign of their outstanding intelligence.

Of course, these magnificent animals are subject to various superstitions, and the white markings were considered indicators of character. Certain white facial markings were deemed to demonstrate the horse's loyalty and endurance, whilst a horse with no white markings was thought to be ill tempered. White socks on the feet were deemed to be good or bad luck, depending on which leg they appeared.

However, it is not just the stimulation of the actual feria that is so appealing, because it is also one of the only times when the flamenco population of Utrera can be found together in one area.

The *Caseta El Mantoncillo* is one of the main rendezvous during the late afternoon, and what will normally start as a recovery period from the previous night's carousing, will often commence into another instantaneous fiesta.

The feria exists solely for the pursuit of pleasure and enjoyment, and the animation of it all is quite irresistible.

However, before one gets too overwhelmed in this four-day whirlwind of self-indulgence, one must remember that the feria also has a somewhat spiritual side.

The fair is dedicated to the *Virgin de la Consolación*, and on the night of September 7, it is traditional to visit her shrine.

123

This white and ochre church was once known as *la Ermita de los Monjes*, because it was a monastery run by a succession of monks; until 1557, when it was left almost abandoned.

The church was then subjected to all kinds of looting and devastation, and this prompted one of the devotees to remove the Virgin from the church and take it to her home for safekeeping.

The arrival, one year later, of a Portuguese monk named Antonio de Santa Maria, saw a restoration of order to the sanctuary, and the virgin was returned to the church under his supervision.

This virgin is now the patron saint of Utrera, and as with most images of the Virgin, La Consolación has a five-hundred year history swathed in legends, fables and miracles.

One of these legends is *El milagro de la lampara de aciete* – 'The miracle of the oil lamp'.

The legend evolves from a cold, stormy night in 1560, when Antonio de Santa Maria is said to have gone, as he did every night, to prey to the virgin. The story claims that when he left the church later that night, he had forgotten to turn off the oil lamp that illuminated the Virgins shrine.

On returning the following morning, he found the lamp still alight and, to his surprise, still full of oil.

Astonished and intrigued by this phenomenon, he decided to leave the lamp burning in order to see for how long it would continue.

The lamp burned continuously without using any oil, but the monk became further astounded by the fact that the virgin's face had begun to change colour.

La Consolación was said to have once been very dark and void of beauty or character, and yet within a couple of days, and without interference of the human hand, she is said to have miraculously become glowing and beautiful.

The seventeenth-century historian, Rodrigo Caro, described her as once being 'very dark and ugly', and yet he was said to have been convinced that her transformation had, in fact, been a miracle.

This icon was carved from pear-wood during the fourteenth or fifteenth century, and these old carvings were called 'black virgins' because they were dark and rather lifeless due to the workmanship and materials used by the artiste of that period.

One of the biggest changes in her physique came about in the baroque period when the virgin, who was originally seated, was reformed into the standing virgin that we see today.

During the late 17th century many of these, unmoving, wooden icons were restored, painted, and clothed in luxurious gowns trimmed with gold and silver. People of wealth and stateliness would donate gold broaches and precious stones to the virgins and La Consolación has been bequeathed numerous jewels from her admires over the years.

La Consolación is the protector of sailors, shippers and merchants, and her shrine has been a place of pilgrimage since the days of Columbus's travels to the new world.

The miracle of the oil lamp attracted even more pilgrims to travel to the shrine, in fact to such an extent that in 1771, King Carlos III tried to ban the pilgrimage on numerous occasions; although without apparent success.

The virgin is rumoured to possess mysterious healing abilities, and this belief will still entice thousands of people to queue for an endless amount of time, in order to touch the virgin and ask for her help or blessing.

A constant flow of people proceeds along the tree lined Paseo de la Consolacíon in hope of receiving some of her miraculous curative powers. Mothers carry sick children, or steady wobbling parents, and the walk to the shrine is a sign of great hope for the grace of reconciliation.

To the right of the church stands the splendid sixteenth century monastery – *Los Minimos*; where by occasion I once had the privilege of listening to the choir of the order rehearsing.

Alonso Alvarez de Albaron designed the portal of the church in 1635, and above the studded wooden door is a stone triptych with mosaic designs of the Virgin de la Consolación flanked by San José and San Joaquin.

Inside, one is confronted with a magnificent baroque altar that covers the entire end wall of the church, and this sixteenth century masterpiece is replete with extravagant gold carvings and overwhelming celestial ornamentation: however, your eyes will automatically rise to the wonderful coffered wood ceiling that is a reminder of the mastery of *Mudejar* carpentry.

Its impressiveness lies not only in the quality of workmanship, but in the fact that it covers the whole nave of the church.

The architect of this masterpiece, Gregorio Tirada, created this incredible ceiling with a polychrome architectural decoration of mathematical precision running along its entire length.

The church is open to the public from midnight on September 7, and thousands of people will flock to the sanctuary in order to make a promise in return for her help.

One of the prettiest, and yet most solemn, rituals takes place in the small courtyard, where people congregate and light tiny candles in remembrance of past loved ones.

The walls of the sacristy are lined with more than four-hundred small paintings, many of which date from the seventeenth century, and some of these are attributed to one of Murillo's disciples[16].

In order to get to the virgin you must pass through the *Sala de Lagarto*. The walls of this somewhat eerie room are decorated with votive offerings left by the devotees, and it is another simple manifestation of the baroque spirit of Andalusia.

I found the atmosphere somewhat peculiar, because the pitifully worn communion gowns gave the room a somewhat deathly fascination.

The room's name derives from the legend of the reptile - *lagarto* - that is said to have appeared from the small well in the middle of the room. A decaying crocodile hangs in shackles above the doorway, although its materialization is obviously far less mysterious than the local myth.

---

[16]Bartolomé Esteban Murillo (Seville 1617 – 1682) was a Spanish baroque painter who is best known for his religious works, but he also painted numerous realist pictures of flower-sellers, street urchins and beggars.

Reptiles feature greatly in Andalusian folklore and whilst snakes are bad omen and somewhat feared by the gypsies, lizards are received as good luck.

It is most probable that this reptile was a gift from the New World, or an allegory left for future generations to speculate over; as is believed to be the case with the crocodile that hangs above the doorway that leads to the *patio de los naranjas* in Seville's cathedral.

The walls of the stair-way that lead to the virgin are lined with dozens of paintings depicting different images of her, and it is with this vast collection that one can see just how much she has altered over time. Whether this has anything to do with the miracle of the oil lamp, or the hands of successive artistes, seems to be categorical, but legends are what continue to fuel the faith.

The arched, polychrome stucco ceiling of the corridor that runs behind the shrine is another *arabesque* work of brilliance, and the vibrant ceiling of the small room that leads to the shrine is a stunning representation of the grandiose fresco murals of this era

The shrine sits high in the altar and looks down on the main hall of the church, and there is barely room to pass by the virgin: one is forced to crouch and squeeze past her ornate temple in order to stand face to face with her.

A continuous flow of people files past the shrine, fumbling with her gold-trimmed robe whilst mumbling the rosary and crossing their selves relentlessly.

The *Virgin de la Consolación* is regarded with the highest esteem, and the belief in her power goes way beyond normal perception.

I have witnessed with my own eyes and ears to what level of regard this town's patron saint is held, and there is one curious incident that may demonstrate the extent of this supremacy.

One night a thief, or thieves, broke into the shrine and stole the small statue of the baby Jesús and most of the virgin's jewels.

The robbery shocked and outraged the entire town and the people were left saddened and confused at such a lowly crime.

It would appear that the culprit may well have been racked with self-reproach, because a few nights after the robbery, the missing objects turned upon the door step of a house in the Calle Porras: the perpetrator was never identified.

THE ESSENCE OF ANDALUSIA

Although I have lived in Andalusia for many years, I am forever amazed at the sheer profundity of the people's faith in the cloth. Having not had a Catholic up-bringing myself, I am frequently confused as to what is taking place during religious celebrations, yet I am often touched by the adoration the Andalusian holds for religious icons.

I felt a sense of fulfilment as I left the sanctuary on the first year that I had attended the pilgrimage to the shrine of La Consolación, and I had even offered my own promise to the virgin: one can only hope in anticipation that the stories of her magical powers have some foundation!

As I walked along the tree lined path and away from the serenity of the church, I was distracted by the shrill of the fair and the loud sevillanas blasting from the casetas on the feria ground.

This feria was only a few hours old, yet the atmosphere was already dripping with the essence of Andalusia.

An array of dazzling dresses of numerous colours and designs adorned the bodies of beautiful women, whose stunning looks were even more alluring than the flamenco dresses they wore.

Blue and red striped canvas marquees, festooned with bunting, paper lanterns and coloured lights, were alive with people drunk on their own adrenalin.

The strains of pure flamenco could be heard coming from some of the packed casetas, whilst others saturated the night air with an infusion of samba and jazz.

The people of Utrera were now officially on holiday because September the eighth is a fiesta; and the celebrations had begun.

The fairground is a maze of colourful casetas that were once owned by individual families, but today companies and consortiums own the majority of them.

El Mantoncillo is owned by a fellowship of flamenco performers and it is one of my favourite haunts during the feria, and it was to be my first port of call on this night.

I had no sooner set foot in the doorway when El Marquesito spotted me and beckoned me to come over to the bar, which was far easier said than done.

The caseta was alive with twirling bodies that engulfed me like lashing waves and the more I tried to reach the bar, the more I was caught in the current of the dancing.

The bar area was also packed to the rafters and the staff fought frantically to serve a barrage of waving arms and empty glasses.

El Marquesito was enjoying a few drinks with Andres de la Carrasca and various other people with whom I am familiar.

Andres is another member from the elongated line of El Pinini and he possesses the archetypical Gypsy characteristics.

I had arrived just in time, because a flamenco recital was about to begin and so after the initial greetings, we stood back and listened to the young Gypsy who began emptying his lungs of some fine cante.

Tables were dragged aside to allow an old woman of around seventy-years of age to demonstrate the simplicity of the Gypsy dance.

No sooner had she returned to her chair, another nimble dame flapped into the space like a fighting hen, and with her skirt hitched above her knees and her bare feet stomping in the dust, she cavorted and teased with utmost gypsyism.

Utrera has its fair share of bohemian type personalities that stand out because of their colourful characters and flamboyant dress sense, and it is these people who often make flamenco so transcendent.

One such character is the aforementioned Andres de la Carrasca, who was, on this occasion, clad in a purple shirt, dark waistcoat, a polka-dotted silk neck-scarf, and a black trilby hat; from which hung his shabby, white ponytail.

With his arms raised high in the air, his hands elegantly twirling as his fingers snapped in time to the rhythm, Andres began to dance in a most buoyant, but truly absorbing, way.

His ability to break into a somewhat ferocious twirl that then decelerated with the elegance of a ballerina, demonstrated that there is a side to this kind of flamenco that cannot be schooled: it is not so important how you dance, so long as you have *compás*.

Compás translates as rhythm, although when used in connection with flamenco it has a much stronger meaning, because it will refer to one's character, grace and knowledge. Traditional village type flamenco does not rely on virtuosity, instead inherent spontaneity is foremost, and it is during this type of gathering that the true masters will prevail over today's academically trained stars.

This fiesta was still going strong at five o clock in the morning: the whiplash clapping and the constant jaleo was the driving force of the flamenco, but it was the continual flow of liquor that stoked the fire and passion of the fiesta.

It is quite amazing that these people never appear to be drunk, especially when one considers the amount of sherry consumed during the feria: tipsy they may be, but never soused.

People drink, and drink often, but they must drink well: one must always be decorous and walk with dignity, since these are crucial qualities of the Andalusian.

Joie de vivre and wit are wholly accepted in these circles, but drunkenness and gauche behaviour are frowned upon, as I once witnessed.

This happened during one of the regular fiestas in Utrera, and the perpetrator had simply consumed far too much whiskey and had begun to make a nuisance of himself.

He was actually quite a good dancer, but the effects of the scotch greatly affected his balance and timing.

Suddenly he began to stumble, and as his legs buckled, he crashed to the floor like an extinguished bull.

I could see that a few of the flamencos were becoming a little uneasy with his behaviour and eventually he was discreetly, yet sternly, told to sit down and calm down; or bugger off!

One question I am often asked concerns the age-old fallacy that the world of flamenco is rife with drugs.

As with any world music, there will be an element of drug abuse, although in my experiences not to the proportion that it is believed to exist.

Flamenco has always had a stigma of ill repute, and this goes back to the eighteenth and nineteenth centuries when private juergas attracted gypsies, prostitutes and low-life.

There have obviously been a few flamenco idols that tarnished flamencos image during the 1970s and '80s, and none so more as the fated Camarón de la Isla or the aptly named Ketama; but this does not mean that the flamenco world is a seedy den of iniquity.

It would be untrue to say that drugs do not exist in the flamenco world, but the few who indulge in the smoking of cannabis, for this is the main form I have witnessed, do so discreetly.

I am fully aware that some of the younger flamencos may use barbiturates or cocaine to fuel long juerga sessions, but it is often the case that it is simply their adrenalin that keeps them going.

The majority of flamencos in Utrera do not need to enhance their minds with drugs, because they are addicted only to their flamenco, and no drug could give a better high than this.

Alcohol on the other hand, does play a moderate role, and although prior to a performance a flamenco will not drink to excess, they will consume enough to 'get them in the mood'.

Copious amounts are drunk during the feria, when these people are at their most relaxed, and they certainly have stamina, and the sense to eat, to endure the long sessions of fiesta.

People were still pouring into the caseta at sunrise, and it seemed that this first night was going to continue for the duration of the feria.

I sneaked off home soon after, because, even though the people of Utrera were on leave, I had to apportion my leisure time with my work.

The following morning I decided to take breakfast in the main square, where a dozen or so people sat outside the only place that was open.

I had arranged to meet a local singer called Pocojato later in the day, so I needed to revitalize my mind and body in order to conduct this interview.

I tried to concentrate on the meeting and prepare some notes and questions to ask the mysteriously named Pocojato, but memories of the previous night's carousing were averting all attempts of concentration. I decided to simply turn up at the meeting and see what transpired.

I still had a few hours before my rendezvous so I decided to venture over to the sanctuary of consolation to see what was transpiring.

A few hours previous the sanctuary had been aglow with candlelight, but now a kaleidoscope of sunrays perpetrated the small stained-glassed windows that are inset high in the walls of the church.

It is far easier to appreciate the splendour of the artwork and decoration of this church during the day, because the true beauty of it all is especially glorious in the natural light.

One of the curious aspects of it all is the fact that not only the old and infirmed flock to this shrine in search of solace. Groups of mixed teenagers and neatly dressed young courting couples also visit in order to pay their respects, and this kind of devotion is what the foreigner so often fails to comprehend.

However, the seriousness of it all is soon replaced by the gayety of the fiesta, because most of these people would soon be indulging in the pleasures of the feria

The feria ground also has a completely different tone during the day, because the un-swept casetas stand motionless and tired-looking: the only sign of life will be the arrival of essential deliveries and replenishments for the coming night's festivities.

I was to return in a few hours to see a performance by a trio called *Pañuelos de Lunares*; whose strangely named singer I was en route to meet.

As I trekked across the empty feria ground and out through the back entrance, I paused to view the shanty- town type dwellings of the street hawkers.

It is a picture of poverty that one might only expect to find in somewhere like Somalia, and the upsetting part is that this unsightly destitution is a stark contrast to the lifestyle taking place on the other side of the fence.

Tarpaulins and plastic sheets held together with crocodile clips and string are erected at the roadside, food is prepared in the street on make shift stoves, and washing lines are suspended between trees and lamp-posts. Half naked children with large glass-like eyes play in the dust and rubble, whilst their parents prepare for another day at the grind.
Most sell African style costume jewelry, wooden carvings or percussion instruments, and they spend their lives following the feria from town to town in order to ply their wares.

FANDANGOS AND FINO

Pocojato is the nickname of Carlos Lopez Nuñéz; a non-gypsy in his late thirties that grew up in the area where the great El Perrate and the humungous family of El Cuchara once lived.

We had arranged to meet in the *Bar Acosta*, which is just a few yards from the hostel, and I must admit to feeling rather alienated on my first visit to this antediluvian haunt.

The long-standing Andalusian existence is most evident in areas like this and there is a hoariness in these old streets that has sadly disappeared from the larger towns and cities.

The dyed-in-the-wool locals use this small bar, and this is the side of Andalusia that the average tourist never comes across: at first, it can seem uninviting or unfriendly, but you will normally find that they are only curious or suspicious because outsiders rarely venture to these parts of the town.

The four old guys that were sat around a small wooden table outside the bar seemed to view me, at first, with some caution, but seeing as I was known to Carlos evidently assured them that maybe I was not so strange after all.

Carlos and I we were soon awash in conversation, however, whilst the meeting was supposed to enlighten me about his life, Carlos seemed more interested in talking about English music and my opinions concerning it. Eventually I managed to steer the conversation in the direction I had originally intended.

Carlos is the youngest of six siblings and although he is not of Gypsy blood, he was raised among some of the greatest Gypsy families of Utrera, and so he is most definitely Gypsy by nature.

His father was a fanatic of flamenco and he loved to sing the fandangos, and Carlos was keen to demonstrate various styles that his father had sung.

His mother, who is affectionately known as Maria La Escalza, still resides in the same streets in which she has spent her entire life.

Carlos talked happily about growing up in these quiet streets, yet he emphasized that the style of living was much different to that of today.

Although their life style was simple, they had wanted little and lived relatively comfortable, or at least to the best of their means. Children would make their own amusement by playing football or mock bullfights and other pass-times that children rarely engage in today.

This was pre- internet and mobile phones, and so if you wanted to know where your friends were, then you'd have to go out into the street and look for them!

Carlos' inner arm is tattooed with the words *pocojato:* on enquiring of its significance, he leant forward onto the table and began to tell the story of his uncle Pepe,

Pepe was known as Pocarropa, which roughly translated means 'few clothes': this would normally indicate that the person only possessed the clothes that he was wearing, but in Pepe's case, the name had been passed down from his father and his grandfather before him.

Carlos had chosen to use the name of Pocojato, which basically means the same, although *jato* is Andalusian dialect for a cloth bag carried on the end of a pole Dick Whittington style. [17]

José (Pepe) Nuñéz Galvan was born in Utrera in 1930 and he appears to have been quite a character, and Carlos took great

[17]Jato will not be found in the Spanish dictionary because it is the andalusian abbreviation of *hatillo;* a small bundle

pleasure in re-living stories concerning his uncle's adventures and shenanigans.

Pepe worked primarily as a farm labourer on a large estate that bordered the land owned by the mayor of Utrera, and the following anecdote demonstrates the socialist nature of many Andalusians of that time.

The labourers that worked for the mayor were well looked after and well fed, where as traditionally, farm labourers lived in pitiful conditions with barely enough food or money to support their families.

The mayor is said to have sanctioned daily supplies to be sent by donkey to his workers, whilst Pepe and his colleagues looked on in envy.

Furious one day that he and his colleagues worked just as hard as anyone else, but had only stale bread to eat, he halted the mule driver and refused him access.

The enraged muleteer told Pepe that he was interfering with the mayor's instructions and ordered him to step aside or face the consequences. But Pepe stood his ground and demanded that as from then on, 'the mayor must send two baskets; one for his own workers, and another for Pocarropa and his comrades'.

Whether the mayor heeded to Pepe's demands, and it appears that he did not, was not of overall importance; the mere fact that he had made a stand was what mattered most.

Whilst Carlos continued unremittingly about his uncle Pepe, a scruffy, bearded old guy suddenly appeared at our table and started nodding his head in my direction and muttering, what I understood to be, obscenities and insults.

His ragged clothes and wild hair had long since been washed or groomed, and his sockless feet squashed down the backs of a pair of tatty carpet slippers.

The vacant look in his eyes indicated that all was not correct inside his head, but I sensed there was no real reason for alarm.

Carlos was familiar with this sadly degenerate and he politely persuaded him to go away and leave us alone to speak.

As he walked away, still chuckling and rambling, the tramp turned back to have one last glance; but what was seen through his craze ridden eyes remains a mystery.

After almost two-hours of exchanging opinions and influences regarding world music - reggae and flamenco in particular - our meeting came to a close.

As we shook hands, I assured Carlos that I would attend the performance of his band later that afternoon, and as I left the bar, my partings were met with the grunts and nods of the curious natives.

A few hours later, back at the feria ground, Carlos introduced me to the other members of *Pañuelos de Lunares*; although I was already familiar with these two sprightly gypsies.

Their music is cluttered with intricate rhythms, stringy guitars and flamenco essence, but because they had been booked for the afternoon session of the feria, today they would have to adhere to the traditional sevillana and rumbas.

I left the caseta at around five-thirty in the afternoon, and whilst taking care not to get trampled by a horse or a cart, I headed over to *El Mantoncillo* to see who had surfaced.

It is at around this hour that the disciples of *Mantoncillo* start to arrive in hordes, and while some look fresh and dazzling in their multihued Andalusian attire; others are red-eyed and tired looking.

I arrived to find Marquesito sitting on a chair outside and looking extremely drained and hung-over: he had continued the previous night's party until eight-thirty in the morning.

Manolito and the rest of the gang also looked a little worse for wear, and the only one of them with any colour in his cheeks was the eighty-two year old El Cuchara.

The mood was very calm and very quiet and El Marquesito's ever-joyful attitude was replaced by a painfully unhealthy tone.
Even his children looked drowsy because they too had watched the sun rise.

El Marquesito talked of his own childhood during the feria, when he would have often been put to sleep on a pile of cushions at the back of the bar, whilst his mother and father sang and danced the night away.

Flamenco is absorbed from a very early age because the children are present during all family get-togethers and celebrations: even in their sleep, they absorb the rhythms of flamenco and, since this is such an everyday way of living, they gain knowledge because they are totally immersed in it at all times.
This caseta would have once attracted the elite of Andalusian flamenco, and the celebrations would continue well into

daylight: it appears that El Marquesito's father, Manuel, would often be the inciter of the fiesta.

Manuel was also known as El Marquesito, and he had taken this noble title from his own father Manuel Nuñéz Reyes - El Marques de Morón.

El Marquesito claims that his grandfather was the legitimate marquis of Morón, because he had acquired the title during a card game that took place Morón de la Frontera during the 1930s.

During this time in Andalusia, it was not unusual for the aristocracy to sell their title in order to pay off a debt, and it would appear that this is how Manuel became El Marques de Morón.

To further endorse this claim, Luis El Marquesito swears to an incident that occurred whilst he was visiting his mother in hospital in Dos Hermanas just prior to her death in 2001.

Whilst having a coffee in the cafeteria of the hospital, El Marquesito claims to have been approached by an ageing gentleman who enquired if he was any relation to El Marques de Morón: the stranger declared that the similarity in their physical characteristics was uncanny.

When his suspicion was confirmed, the old guy continued to say that he had in fact been present during the infamous card game in which Manuel Nuñéz had won the title.

El Marquesito claims to have never met this man before, and yet the stranger had recognized him instantly. This clarifies, said he, that the story concerning his grandfather's title was genuine.

I was struggling to hear what El Marquesito was saying about his grandfather, because of the mayhem created by dozens of children that ran boisterously in and out of the caseta, and all attempts to calm them were futile.

All of the sudden, like a bolt out of the sky, a tennis ball struck El Marquesito on the side of the head with the force of a fist; sending his drink flying from his hand.

His face turned thunderous as he swung around on his seat to see what had in fact just hit him with such might.

By now, of course, the young lad who had launched it had scarpered into the caseta and, thankfully, out of range of the torrent of obscenities that was unleashed into the warm summer's night air.

The rest of the group could not control their gleefulness and fell about their seats, whilst El Marquesito rubbed his head and looked for some sort of sympathy; which obviously he went without.

The mood began to change an hour or so later, when the Barcelona branch of the Marquesito family descended on the caseta en-masse.

El Marquesito had not seen them for more than four years and so the initial arrival was met with animated salutations and much hugging, kissing and tears.

There are, at present, around two-hundred members of the Pinini clan living in Barcelona: their parents had left Andalusia at the end of the nineteen-sixties in hope of better work prospects.

Antonio, the elder of the group, began tapping the rhythm of the buleria on the bar top with such force, the plates of cheese and flutes of sherry began bouncing along the counter.

Antonio sang of his happiness at returning to his homeland, and the rapping knuckles and flicking fingers of the rest of the group soon gained the attention of all present: what started as a simple burst of happiness, quickly progressed into a frenzy of heated Gypsy mayhem.

The contentment and elation that invaded this small corner of the caseta was overwhelmingly emotional, and whilst the men mindlessly danced and sang, their stunning women goaded them with equal enthusiasm.

Esperanza, the wife of El Marquesito, is strikingly good-looking, with a fine cheekbone structure, the eyes of a nervous stallion, olive-brown skin, and the aura of a mythical goddess.

Bejewelled with large dangling earrings and costume trinkets of dazzling design, Esperanza has the complexion and characteristics that artist's fall over themselves to paint.

This fiesta really got going when a young Gypsy lad, of no more than thirteen years of age, presented himself to El Marquesito. He wanted to sing fandangos, and we quickly learned of the boy's incredible ability to sing pure flamenco.

With no guitarist at hand, this young Gypsy had only the clapping hands of his audience to accompany him, and this included some of the mightiest names of flamenco: this did not deter him and his obvious youth disappeared with his aged style of singing.

Wriggling and twisting on his seat as he sang, his face changing from heart-felt passion to cheeky-boy grin, he soon had his audience eating out of his hand.

This was flamenco in its most natural habitat, and the sudden outburst of song in situations such as these, will demonstrate the unfeigned significance of the art.

And so they danced and sang, and as the *manzanilla* wine flowed, the fiesta gained momentum; and yet it was only just seven o clock in the afternoon.

Gone are the days when I could party from dusk till dawn and I learned long ago the importance of taking a break in order to eat something hot and maybe rest for half an hour.

I decided to slip away to grab forty winks and then prepare for the coming night; leaving the Marques's occupied with their jubilant reunion.

A siesta at this hour is often an impossible task, and any thought of one on this particular afternoon quickly diminished at the sound of hammers, drills and cement mixers engaged in the renovation of the house opposite my window.

This is to say nothing of un-silenced scooter exhausts, car horns, and the screeching of women who shout to each other across the narrow streets.

A few hours later I arrived at the caseta *Inés y Luis*; fully recharged and rearing to go.

Inés Suarez Jiménez and her brothers Luis and Antonio administer this caseta, and because they are relations of La Fernanda and La Bernarda de Utrera, it is always the scene of much nostalgia.[18]

Only a mere few of Pinini's grandchildren are still alive, and they are rarely seen in this caseta today, but many of his great-grandchildren and their families will be found here on most nights of the feria.

This caseta is also the favourite haunt of my good friend Manuel Requelo and this is where he spends the nights with his large family and numerous friends.

On this night, as is normal, Manuel leapt from his seat and greeted me in his usual manner, and then set about organizing a large ice bucket containing two bottles of Tio Pepe. He then informed me that I was in for an unusual treat later on; although he did not reveal what it was.

155

---

[18]The correct, and rather long, name of this caseta is *Inés y Luis y sobrinos de Fernanda y Bernarda*

I am always treated like one of the family, and indeed I feel that way, and time spent with the Requelos is seldom an uneventful occasion.

It is somewhat difficult to spend money during the feria and this occasion was no exception, because my efforts to buy a round were squashed every time I attempted.

To be invited into a caseta is similar to being invited into their home, and it can occasionally be taken as an insult if you insist on paying your way.

Eventually I had to artfully pay the barman for a bottle of Tio Pepe, whilst no one else was watching, but even he was reluctant to accept my money, and Manuel became quite infuriated when he realized what I had done.

My attention was momentarily distracted by a 'no smoking' sign that hung behind the bar, which enforced my belief that the bans that have been introduced throughout Europe, would not have the same effect in Spain as they appear to have had elsewhere.

Although the majority of bars and restaurants in Spain are complying with these laws, there are, in certain places, bars where the customers are allowed to smoke.

One of the ways around the ban - and if there is a loop-hole the Spanish will find it – is to claim the establishment is a *socio* - or members only club. Although there is no membership fee, registration, or committee of any kind, it is, at present, a way to sidestep the law.

Most people will agree that smoking in restaurants has been banned for the right reasons, so I won't go on too much, but I am inclined to believe that there are certain times when these laws seem trivial.

Most of the casetas I visited allowed smoking, and yet they all had the signs to remind us that it was in fact illegal to light up inside, but few people, including the staff, took much notice of them.

The outspoken, and much respected, Spanish film director Luis Buñuel once claimed that "it is impossible to drink without smoking".

Although I am an admirer of Buñuel, I would not totally agree with this, but I do believe that for people who do enjoy both, there are times when the two are simply made for each other.

I once asked one senior bar owner, who had worked his establishment for more than fifty years, if he was not worried of incurring a heavy fine for allowing his customers to light up inside the bar. He answer was simple.

He claimed that many of his customers were also his friends and that they had been frequenting his bar for many years in order to drink coffee or wine, play dominoes, and smoke. He had seen a considerable decline in clientele over the past few years because of the recent recession that had taken a grip on the country, and he was slowly going under.

If he should prohibit them from smoking they would not come anymore and he would for sure lose the business anyway, so it was better to take a chance, than destroy it himself.

The treat that Manuel had previously mentioned, came in the shape of a small Croatian musician known as *Pepe el Trompeta,* who, for reasons unknown, had been absent from the feria for the past few years.

This multitalented Gypsy musician had been serenading the audiences of the casetas in Utrera for many years, and for this he has become legendary. He has made a few recordings and these discs can occasionally be found in the CD racks that are found outside many of the tourist gift shops in Seville.

He is celebrated for his unique skill of playing the trumpet with one hand, whilst clanking a keyboard of an organ with his other: his exciting and visual styles of sevillana had people spinning and jiving, as his music rattled around the room with the force of a Balkan wedding band.

It was impossible for anyone to sit, or stand, still as Pepe shouted and danced as he played, and it appeared as though he would never stop because he was having such a good time himself.

So fast and ferocious was his music, one could barely catch a breath, and when Pepe and trumpet had disappeared into the night, we were left floating back down to our seats.

Soon the music started up again, only this time it was supplied by the huge sound system that belted out the tunes of a young Inés y Luis.

This brother and sister duo had once excited audiences all over Spain with their catchy rumba-flamenco, but today both are resigned to the odd appearance at the *Potaje Gitano* festival or a family fiesta.

Luis is now in his sixties and his boyish image of the nineteen seventies has been replaced by the haggard look of an aging rock-star.

On this night, he sat motionless in the corner of the caseta, surveying the scenes and sipping on his glass of sherry, until a young lad who leapt into the centre to perform roused his somewhat stupefied look.

It would appear, from the way he performed, that what he did was for the sole attention of Luis, because he danced in front of him like a courting peacock may try to attract a hen.

Had he been able to channel his energy and contain his eagerness to impress, he would have had the makings of a good dancer, but true flamenco is a spontaneous release and not a swaggering demonstration of one's talent.

It was hard to decipher if the look of sheer astonishment on the face of Luis was in appreciation of his gestures, or bemusement of them.

I could see that it was fast approaching daylight and so decided to take the opportunity to slide off home before sunrise.

My offers of appreciation and gratitude for such a wonderful night were interrupted by yet another noisy group of musicians, who burst into the caseta like a Dixieland marching band.

These guys are as traditional to the feria, as are horses and Sherry, and the pounding drums and crashing cymbals drive rousing trumpets, saxophones and tubas. Again, the caseta erupted into a sea of cavorting bodies, whilst the musicians danced in and around them, blowing their horns and chanting with joy.

As I snuck out of the caseta and headed home, I passed the bullring, where thousands of youngsters were engaged in the traditional *botellon,* and although this massive street-party looked rather inviting, I decided my feria had come to an end.

AIRS OF ANDALUSIAN ROME

The bullfight is probably the one aspect of Spanish life that most foreigners find hard to understand, and the majority maintain that it is just a barbaric exhibition of Spanish blood-lust.

Opinions concerning the contest differ considerably in today's utterly correct world, and this is one aspect of Spanish life that raises much passion, both for, and against.

The bullfight is generally perceived to have originated in Rome and theories abound that the spectacle was introduced to Hispania by the Emperor Claudius: he is said to have proposed it as a substitute for the gladiators.

The gladiator, latin for 'swordsman', engaged in violent confrontations with both man and beast, and the ritual was established on the conception of fighting, and dying, with honour: the bullfight of today is based on the same concept.

It is perhaps hard for a non-aficionado to comprehend that the person who respects the bull the most is the one who is going to end its life.

This is one subject that is best avoided, rather like politics and religion, because unless you are familiar with the whole ritual, you will never accept it for what it is.

It is certainly an area of Spanish culture that needs to be approached with great knowledge, because Spaniards are not interested in the opinions of 'uneducated' protesters.

I am neither an expert, nor an avid aficionado, but I do have a respect of the animal and an equal regard of the *torero*.[19]

My conscience had first been plagued by my love of animals and dislike of blood-sports, but I soon learned that this art involved much more than an inequitable slaying.

This chapter however, is not designed to discuss the wrongs and rights of the bullfight; it is simply another aspect of Spanish life that I came into close contact with. My views and opinions respect a tradition that has been part of the Spanish establishment for hundreds of years, and I believe that the furture of bullfighting should be left in the hands of the Spanish people.

164

---

[19]Torero means a fighter of bulls and refers to all participants of the cuadrilla, regardless of the individual's role: to declare 'soy torero' is said with enormous dignity.

The ranches where these bulls are raised - *ganaderias* - are like small fortresses with high walls that are guarded night and day: these animals are sacrosanct and must be protected from molestation by inquisitive intruders, because the bull's memory is prodigious.

The entire premise of the bullfight is established on the fact that, other than a basic necessity during its early years, the bull will never before have faced a man on foot.

The *toro bravo* is a remarkable blend of power, agility, and intensifying intelligence, and he uses his horns with lethal efficiency.

The bull's first brief encounter with man comes at around nine-months, when he is branded, numbered, and named. His second comes at the age of two during the ceremony of the *tienta*.

The tienta is another fascinating ritual in the social-life of the Andalusians and yet it is one of the few aspects of this life that is not openly shared with outsiders.

The young bulls are confronted by a horseman – *garrochista* - armed with a lance, and it is his job to check that the animal is valiant.

The bull should charge at the unfamiliar intruder without hesitation and on doing so the garrochista will lightly prick the bull between the shoulder blades, to which, he is expected to retaliate. If he does, his name and number is recorded and his destination is the plaza.

I once witnessed the immense skill involved in this procedure and I quickly realised that it was not simply the case of a horseman agitating the bull with a spear, for the garrochista must understand the bull to the extent of being able to manipulate it.

On this occasion, the garrochista spoke to the animal in a way in which it appeared to understand, and he could command the bull to do certain things using simple gestures with the lance.

These sprawling ranches will always have a small bullring where young bulls will engage in a series of entertaining bullfights, but the confrontations will be brief.

These bullfights may be performed by famous matadors, budding amateurs desperately trying to demonstrate their worth, or friends with simple affection for the bull. There is a kind of greenhorn quaintness in this ceremony that makes one overlook the fact that these animals are being trained to be killed, and because the young bulls are often alert, excited and eager to perform; the spectacle has a kind of playful ambience.

However, this ritual is not solely for entertainment, and neither is it a chance to show off, because it is also one of the only times that a young aspirant gets to practise his trade.

Young hopefuls once travelled for miles on foot in the expectation of an invitation to participate in this ritual, and even today, this is an area that is extremely hard to break into without the necessary connections.

Previous to the tienta, the young apprentice's only encounter with a set of horns would have come from mock training sessions. One boy would charge at the opponent with a pair of horns attached to a piece of wood, thus giving the apprentice a chance to practise his moves and turns; in privacy he would attain grace and posture in front of a mirror.

Manolito de Angustias was one of the people who helped me understand what the bullfight is actually about and it was he who first offered to accompany me to the plaza de toros in Utrera.

I felt excited by the prospect of my first bullfight, and yet rather nervous: would I turn my head away from the final thrust of the sword? There was a chance that I might leave the arena after the first kill, but in order to fully absorb the spectacle, I would try to do neither.

I did however spend the entire day veering from excitement to apprehension about the forthcoming melee, but I needn't have fretted, because this first occasion fell foul to the curse of the fiesta.

There were a few occasions when plans had been set in motion to attend the bullfight in Utrera, although these could easily be, and often were, derailed at the last minute because another celebration had dictated otherwise.

Utrera did not have a bullring for many years and even now, with a new six-thousand-seat stadium, *corridas* are limited to the week of the feria.

The new bullring had been at the centre of some confusion for many years and there was a period when it seemed that Utrera might never have another bullring.

The old one, which was in a state of decay, was eventually demolished in 2002, even though there was much protestation at its closure.

After years of debating whether Utrera actually needed a bullring, permission for its construction was eventually approved and it finally opened its doors during the feria of 2010.

It is hard to understand why the council of a town that has been a supreme source of the toro bravo, should occasionally juggle with Utrera's bullfight heritage.

More recently, a storm blew up because of an announcement made by the city council, which declared its intentions to introduce a ban on children under the age of seven from entering the bullring.

The bullfight has suffered greatly through the recent financial crisis and attempts have been made to lure aficionados back by way of reduced fees for the unemployed and students, and free entry for children under the age of five.

The proposal to restrict children under seven would deprive would-be young bullfighters from gaining the early introduction that is necessary, as most begin their initial preparation when four or five years old.

Of course, the new legislation was met by several protests organized by the local bullfighting sector, and it would appear that these plans have since been swept to the bottom of the importance pile.

I always imagined that the bullfight in Utrera would have the same age-old atmosphere that seems impregnated into every aspect of the town, and my supposition was soon endorsed.

However, on entering this huge stadium one is devastated by the unattractiveness of its bland concrete structure, for it certainly lacks the beauty of the Maestranza bullrings in Seville and Ronda, but when the auditorium is occupied and the presentation begings, the ugliness of the edifice is subdued in the entire tumult of it all.

Elegantly dressed children of just two or three years of age are perched on the shoulders of their proud fathers, while groups of men in their senior years are huddled around wiskey flasks and wine skins.

The atmosphere is one of complete vibrancy and one can see how easy it is to succumb to the bullfight, becoming enthralled in the multihued, razzmatazz ambience of this society.

Manolito had previously advised me that, although the privilege of watching the fight from behind the *barrera* could be quite a thrilling experience, it would be wiser for a first-timer to sit further back: this way one is less vunerable to shock, and the smell of blood.

Six apprentice bullfighters - *novilleros* - were to perform and four of these were from Utrera; needless to say, there was a sociable ambience in the air.

This type of bullfight is a show case of the younger talent that is hoping to break into the professional levels of the art, and so, because there were no famous names on the cartel, the entrance fee was kept reasonably low: I suspect that this was another reason for the good turnout.

There is a sense of nervous tension as the spectators wait for the president's gesture, and when he finally gives the signal, the gate will swing open and the toreros and their entourage enter the ring, and the mood becomes elevated.

The toreros, gorgeously dressed in the dazzling gold-trimmed suits, march abreast to the centre of the ring, their *cuadrillas* also in line behind them, and the band swing into the traditional *pasodoble*.

This is a marvelous moment as the entourage moves across the arena, led by two picturesque horsemen called *alguaciles*. These are the marshals and they are clad in 17th century black costume complete with gaudy plumes sprouting from their hats: one of these marshals will then dismount and act as the relayer of the president's orders, and he will also supervise the cutting of such trophies as he sanctions.

The brigade is followed by two mules, whose job it is to drag the dead bulls from the plaza.

After the routine tour of the ring and acknowledgment to the president, who observes everything fom his box high above the arena, the mood becomes more relaxed.

The matadors stroll to the red-painted, chest-high, barrier in order to remove their dress cloaks and collect their heavy fighting capes, which have been placed over the barrier in readiness.

For the next few minutes the six young bullfighters, and the members of their cuadrilla, practise their turns and passes like clock-work toys; their crimson and yellow capes flowing in graceful synchronization and their sequined suits shimmering in the sunlight.

Moments later the sound of the bugles signals the opening of the toril gates and within seconds the first huge bull bounds out at a brisk canter, looking alert and ready to play.

At first he sees no-one because the bullfighters are hidden behind the the wooden shield – *burladero* - that the matador will often dash to for protection, but eventually one torero emerges and the bull spots the flapping of the cape, and charges without hesitation.

There is something delightful about the bull in these early stages because it appears to be a game, but he quickly learns why he is now in this ring.

Each novillero has to fight one bull, and all six of these fine-looking beasts were strong, alert and extremely dangerous, and any first thoughts one has about their adorability are quickly diminished.

There is a sense of amateurishness about these fights, but it is certainly a good way to learn about the art, because much of the realness of the art is often lost in flashy showmanship.

One aspect that particularly intrigued me was the act of the *banderillero*, because the placing of these longdarts seemed to be far more dangerous than any of the work with the cape.

When the bull charges, it is the cape that he sees and tries to destroy, but the banderillero has no cape and is rather vunerable, and it is quite simply his precise timing and nimbleness that keep him from a goring.

When done correctly, this part of the fight is one of the most entertaining, and yet it takes on an air of comedy as the banderillero sprints away from the angered animal.

Before the torero can kill, he must first seek the permission of the president, after which he will perform a ritual known as the *brindis*, or the salute.This action descends directly from the the gladiators cry: - 'We who are about to die salute you'.

The torero approaches the president's box with his hat held high in his direction and after he is acknowledged, turns to salute his spectators.

At this stage his hat might be tossed to someone in the crowd, but on this occasion, after he had rotated with the grace of a musical-box ballerina , it was placed on the sand of the arena.

If a torero decides to dedicate a bull to someone, he will hand, or gently throw, his hat to that person, but he will only do this if he is sure he can perform well with that particular bull.

If he chooses to dedicate it to the public, he will stand in the center of the ring and slowly pivot a full circle, hat in right hand saluting the crowd. He will then throw the hat over his shoulder.

However, superstition dictates that if it falls upside down he will have bad luck with that bull; hence, some of the more superstitious matadors place the hat on the ground the right way up in order to make certain.

After, what were obviously, some fine moves, the band struck up and the crowd went wild. The bull looked confused as to why he could not get his opponent, but continuusly charged with head down and snout rubbing in the sand.

Of course, when you witness this first-hand for the first time, you realize just how dangerously close the bulls horns come to the matador's body.

The first kill of the afternoon was by no means perfect and the bull continued to attack the toreros long after the sword had been badly placed: the second thrust was as instant as a bullet and the bull was extinguished immediately.

For someone who is 'on the fence' with regard to the corrida, I feel sure that the 'killing' is far more stomachable if it is done properly.

I believe that it is every matador's intention to achieve this, but I also understand that it is something that you will be very lucky to witness today.

One will rarely witness a kill in which the bull is dead by time it appears from the underside of the *muleta;* as in the days of Belmonte and Manolete.

The most curious act is carried out after the kill, when the spectators engage in the strange ritual of shaking handkercheifs and protesting to the president in favour of a reward for the torero.

This bizzare outburst is, so it seems, all part of the customary audience participation, but it was executed with the utmost commotion by the noise loving, fiery tempered spectators.

There were a few near misses, and the bull occasionally got the better of the torero, and these were to provide a few adrenalin rushes for me.

One of the toreros was tossed in the first few minutes of the contest, but fortunately he was saved from serious injury by the quick-thinking members of his cuadrilla, and the young apprentice was soon back on his feet.

This type of tossing is called a *cogida*, which is a mishap where the torero is tossed, but not gored. Thankfully there were no *cornadas,* a more serious incident where the torero is gored, but the near-misses gave one an idea of how dangerous this profession can be.

It is no wonder that all bullrings have a chapel that the bullfighters will visit before entering the ring.

In these last few moments before facing the horns, most matadors will feel nervous and isolated and they know full well that these might be the last prayers that they ever utter. One cannot imagine what is going through the matador's mind as he enters the ring, and although he seems to revel in the adulation that greets him, in just a few moments his mind will be devoid of anything other than survival.

I am still somewhat undecided about my feelings towards the bullfight. If I am honest, there is still a part of me that does not like the spectacle, and yet I uphold the utmost respect for this long-standing tradition. Although I feel I will never become an avid aficionado of the bullfight, there is something about the characteristics and environment associated with this art that I find impossible to ignore.

Rosemary will with you go

Andalusia is a land of passion, pain and intense, vibrant color, and even though the Andalusian likes to celebrate life to the extreme, they have a somewhat bizarre fascination with death.

Death is romanticized in the fairy tale world of poets like Federico Garcia Lorca; who once claimed that a dead man is more alive as a dead man in Spain, than anywhere else in the world.

The *granadino* poet associated strongly with the duende, claiming it to be an 'irrational, demonic, death seeking spirit, without which, deep inspiration was impossible'.

He also claimed that duende was only possible when one sensed that death was imminent, but when one considers the reverie world in which Lorca based his work; one can see how duende became a kind of incomprehensible, intangible spirit.

The duende, in my experiences, is most often associated with the cante flamenco, and even though it can be induced by the dance, the solo guitar, and even the bullfight, it will usually be the broken voice of a Gypsy singer that inspires this indefinable occurrence.

Certain singers will possess 'duende', and yet it is not a quality or technique that one acquires with practice or dexterity; it is a presence which is beckoned from the deep abyss in which it lies. It is like wind, for you will know when it materializes and, although you cannot see or touch it, you will sense its overwhelming presence.

It was once, and still is to some extent, customary to sing siguiriyas and soleares at a wake, or a funeral, and these chilling styles of cante are most proficient at inducing the duende.

As with a saeta sung to the images of the passion during Holy Week, the siguiriyas are sung with immeasurable sentiment, and when sung at a funeral, when emotions are at their most disorientated, the duende can often be experienced.

Funerals are never joyous occasions, and yet the first catholic funeral that I had attended is an experience that has been fixed in my memory, simply because of the theatrical scenes that unfolded during it.

The funeral was preceded by the habitual twenty-four hour vigil in the chapel of rest, and the coffin had been left open in order for the family to say their last goodbyes.

I had never viewed a corpse before this time, and I had no real wanting need to do so on this occasion either, but the deceased was a member of my extended Spanish family, so I felt compelled to do what was undoubtedly expected of me.

The mourner's spoke of the deceased as one may speak of a sleeping baby in a cot; smiling sorrowfully and repeatedly avowing how happy and beautiful he now looked.

At first I quickly glimpsed without really seeing, and my eyes were drawn to the floral tributes, and not the body: when I did eventually affix my eyes on the corpse, there was something surreal about it all.

The abundance of floral color surrounding the open-top casket, and the serene face of the deceased, reminded me of something that Freda Kahlo may have painted.

The mood was calming and quite relaxed, until the deceased's elder sister arrived: no sooner had she entered the room, the wailing began and the whole scene became a howling mass of hysteria: the men hardly raised an eyebrow, other than to suggest acknowledgment of the spectacle.

Once inside the chapel, the sister fell to her knees, bawling and crying out uncontrollably as the priest conducted the service, and as the coffin was carried from the church, she clung to it in a discomforting display of melodramatic anguish. Funerals are never enjoyable and the atmosphere at this stage was by no means pleasurable, but there was an air of melodramatic travesty in much of her tragic display.

In Andalusia, and especially in Seville, this type of mourner is often referred to as *'los de la mantiitas'*, because along with the habitual black attire and veil covered faces, they will bring small blankets – mantitas - to keep them warm whilst they keep a vigil over the body throughout the night prior to the funeral.

The vigil is a custom that has almost disappeared from Andalusia today, but there are still many of the older generation that adheres to this ritual: they believe it to be disrespectful to abandon the deceased before the internment, and so they will spend the entire night weeping and groaning over the corpse.

A funeral in Utrera is obviously a somber event, and yet, because the majority of the town is related, there is an intimacy and solidarity that creates a less solemn ambience.

The funeral of Fernanda Jiménez Peña – La Fernnanda de Utrera - was one of the grandest Utrera had seen for many years and the service had an air of stateliness, which was nothing more than expected for such a revered woman.

Politicians interrupted their sessions to acknowledge the passing of this celebrated singer, and television personalities, musicians and matadors remembered her with such tenderness[20].

The funeral service of her sister, La Bernarda de Utrera, was held in the church of *Santiago el Mayor*, during which the priest described Bernarda as the complement of her sister – 'like cotton and silk'[21].

Some of the younger members of the Pinini family acted as pallbearers, and as the coffin left the church, draped in a mantle of the *Virgin de la Consolacíon*, hundreds of people cheered and applauded Bernarda as she went on her last journey through the streets of Utrera.

183

The funeral procession passed by the monument dedicated to the sisters, before continuing to her final resting place in the municipal cemetery; although, as the priest had suggested, Bernarda was already in heaven with Fernanda, and most likely singing at a Gypsy fiesta.

---

[20]Fernanda Jimenéz Peña died in Utrera on 24 - 08 - 2006

[21]Bernarda Jimenéz Peña died in Utrera on 28 - 10 - 2009

There were of course tears, but they were shed discreetly and without the howling and anguish so often associated with a funeral in Spain.

Their tomb had been donated by the local council and it was another simple offer of generosity in the memory of these two much worshipped woman.

By strange circumstance, even though Fernanda had died three years previous, Bernarda would be the first to occupy the tomb because it had only recently been finished. The family has since made the difficult decision to have Fernanda's body disentombed and placed in the new shrine so that the sisters would rest together for eternity.

Opened in the 19th century with the funding of Clemente de la Cuadra, the municipal cemetery in Utrera demonstrates the kind of affluence and affection that is evident in most aspects of the town. [22]

---

[22] One of the most respected names associated with Utrera is that of Don Clemente de la Cuadra (1803 - 1873); the patriarch of an extremely wealthy and culturally educated family whose resources were used to enrich the town.

With the mandate and funding of Don Clemente, major public works were carried out and he became the protagonist of numerous projects in the town.

It is located on the opposite side of the railway tracks and is rather awkward to access on foot, even though it is visible from the train station.

A high ochre colored wall that runs around the perimeter is entered through a small arched doorway, which leads into the Patio de San Francisco.

What most removes the gloomy idea of death from the mind is the exuberant ornamentation that confronts you when entering the cemetery.

The walls are set with niches, one above the other like filing cabinets, whilst in the gardens, amongst the cypresses, are the white marble tombs of those who could afford a more regal form of burial.

This is the oldest part of the cemetery and some of the tombs are crumbling and neglected, whilst others are affronted with pristine marble plaques engraved in gold leaf and inset with photographs of the departed.

The catacomb of the mystical La Serneta is located in this part of the cemetery, but time has almost erased the name of whose bones it contains.

A small chapel is tucked away in the corner of the patio and is barely visible until one is upon it. It is in a pitiful state and overgrown with weeds and bushes, and although at present it is simply crumbling to the ground, there are plans to renovate it sometime in the future.

One of the most prominent mausoleums is that of the Perrate family, which sits in the garden of the central patio. This spotless, white marble shrine is beautifully sculptured and consists of a large square tomb decorated with a marble guitar draped with a shawl.

The celebrated El Perrate was laid to rest here along with his wife Tomasa, and a few of their children who met with premature deaths. This is one monument in the cemetery that is obviously tended with loving care on a regular basis.

Not all of the tombs are as decorative as this one, and many of them are rather awkward to distinguish because of their simplicity.

One would have no problem in finding the tomb of Gaspar de Utrera though, since there is a picture of his face imposed onto the marble crypt.

When viewing this tomb it is easy to forget that it contains just the dust and bones of this great man, because his smiling countenance portrays a fullness of life.

Utrera's flamenco population have been honored to the very end and even with the finality of death, it seems as though they have never actually left.

On the other side of the garden there is another large mausoleum, and although this is not as ornamented as the tomb of El Perrate, it has a kind of regal stateliness that reveals it contains someone very important. This huge bulk of marble is the kind of tomb normally assigned to royalty or nobility, and the neat circular garden that surrounds it is fragranced by hundreds of tiny rosemary plants.

The names of Fernanda and Bernarda de Utrera are carved onto the top of the marble tomb and there seems to be tranquility in this small circular garden: although cemeteries are never the liveliest of places, the aura surrounding their tomb is almost celestial.

Two fir trees have been cultivated and shaped so that they join like a symbol of the sister's inseparableness, and the potent smell of rosemary reminds one of the plants long associations with death.

The aromatic rosemary bush has a history that stretches back thousands of years and it is steeped in the practices and myths of many a varied civilization.

Its Spanish name is *romero,* or pilgrims plant, and this name is believed to derive from the legend about the Virgin Mary's cloak.[23]

It has long been recognized as a symbol of respect and remembrance, and in many parts of Europe a sprig of rosemary would once have been tossed into the coffin of the deceased.

It has been found in Egyptian tombs dating from as far back as 3000 BC, and in Spain, the placing of a sprig in the hands of the departed was a symbol that the dead would not be forgotten.

Travelers would often wear it in their lapels when journeying the dangerous highways of Andalusia, because it was believed to ward of witch-craft and menaces.

George Borrow mentioned these superstitions in 1843 when he claimed a Gypsy woman gave him a sprig of rosemary to

---

[23] The Virgin Mary was said to have hung her cloak over a rosemary bush in the Egyptian desert and when she removed the cloak, the tiny white flowers had miraculously turned the same color blue as her cloak.

wear in his hat because she feared for his safety. If we are to believe his book, *The bible in Spain*, it did little to protect Borrow from the hazards of the roads at that time.

Along with its ability to prolong youthfulness, enhance memory, bring luck in love and marriage, not to mention its mystical healing powers, the gypsies of Andalusia believe that rosemary wards off evil.

It should come as no surprise as to why the Gypsy fortune-tellers, who ply their trades around most cathedrals and places of tourist attraction in Spain, tempt you with the offer of a sprig of rosemary.

Once accepted, you will not only be badgered into having your palm read for an extortionate fee, but you will be told never to dispose of the rosemary other than by burning.

Gypsies and fire have shared a long supernatural connection, and yet the traditional Romany custom concerning burial avoided cremation, because their custom dictates that the body must be returned to the earth.

The deceased's belongings, and even their caravan, would be burnt though, because they believed it bad luck to possess a dead man's belongings. This ritual obviously removed the possibility of family disputes concerning the deceased's possessions; a practice most of society may do well to consider.

The Gypsy funeral, like the wedding, is a large affair and the main aim is to ensure that the deceased will be given the best possible send off on their final journey: they believe it is imperative that the spirit leaves this world happy.

In general, the gypsies are very spiritual and many believe that they are watched over by the presence of their ancestors; some believe that these spirits guide them along life's journey.

THE SPIRIT OF UTRERA

I have long had a burning desire to reimburse the people of Utrera for the continual support and friendship they have shown me over the years.

Utrera has made such an impact on my life and I feel that my association with this town has enriched my cultural awareness to a level I may never have otherwise acquired.

I believe that any town that has such a grand cultural history, and one that has played such a huge role in the promotion of their talent, must surely be accredited with the utmost respect.

I have often thought that Utrera should be accorded more worldwide recognition than it currently receives because, although the town is firmly engraved into the history of flamenco, it is relatively unknown outside of Spain.

I tried to show a little consideration for the town by presenting in Utrera the Spanish version of the book about El Pinini, but even this event was largely organized and instigated by the people of Utrera.

It seemed that whenever I wanted, or needed, to do something in this town, the floodgates would open and I would find myself bombarded with offers of help.

Utrera is not, however, associated solely with flamenco, because the town has a lucrative cultural history and is also, amongst many things, the birthplace of two of Spain's most distinguished writers; *Los Hermanos Quinteros*.

Serafin Álvarez Quintero and his brother, Joaquin, were born in Utrera in 1871 and 1873 respectively, and they wrote over two-hundred plays; winning them fame as the 'golden boys' of the Madrid theatre.

Their father, Joaquin Álvarez Hazañas, an affluent gentleman wealthy enough to allow his sons to choose a theatrical career and one-time mayor of Utrera, was said to have had an affair with La Serneta; the celebrated Gypsy flamenco singer who once lived in the town.

This subject has fuelled an unrelenting debate that has continued for many years, yet we are no closer to the truth, and as I have already covered the life of La Serneta in a previous book, I feel it unnecessary to discuss the matter further in this one.

One of Spain's most infamous bandits, Diego Corrients Mateos, was born in Utrera in 1757: the kind of *banderlero* who stole from the rich and gave to the poor, he was eventually captured and hanged in Seville in 1781.

After his execution, Corriente's body was dismembered and sent to the different provinces where he had been active.

His head, which was buried in the *Iglesia de San Roque* in Seville, was found last century during restoration work to the church.

Francisco Ruiz Gijón, a prominent Spanish sculptor, famed for his highly ornamented effigies, was born in Utrera in 1653. Although he went to Seville as a child, following the death of his father, Guijón is still closely associated with Utrera.

One of his most recognized effigies is the tormenting carving of *El Cachorro,* the Christ of expiration, which was supposedly inspired by the violent cessation a young Gypsy.

The Gypsy, known as *El Cachorro,* had been stabbed by the enraged husband of the woman whom he had been carrying on with.

Bending over the dying Gypsy, the artiste felt the warmth of his last breath as it left the body, and observed the boy's black pupils in their final gaze.

This was the image he had so longed to, and eventually did, create; a face that imparts maximum agony and a remarkable countenance of death.

This barely touches the surface of Utrera's cultural wealth and yet one may begin to see why this town has spun such a magical web around me.

Of course, my first attraction was, and always will be, the gypsies and their flamenco, but I soon found that most of the town's social history seemed to go hand in hand with them.

The town is unquestionably not short of flamenco legends, quite the opposite in fact. They have certainly produced some of the performers who truly demonstrate the true meaning of this art, and one need look no further for better advocates of it.

One day I was presented with an opportunity to prove this point. I would also have a chance to throw a spotlight on the town, and give something back to Utrera, although again, in a less significant proportion than the debt I owe.

This opportunity came one spring morning when I received a telephone call from the BBC in England, for they wanted to make a documentary about flamenco and I was asked if I would be interested in assisting with the production.

The show was to be made in two parts and the first section was based on the life and work of the Cordovan guitarist, Paco Peña.

The second section was to focus on the Gypsy-flamenco way of life and how flamenco assists their daily routines: it was also to focus on the role of flamenco during Semana Santa.

I was to organize a meeting of various singers and a guitarist in order to record them talking about their flamenco, and also capture their art during a spontaneous juerga.

I had to arrange a venue where this could all be achieved, and this location had to be in a town that had some kind of spiritual connections with the gypsies and their music: the one town where I could almost certainly accomplish all of this was Utrera.

The recording was to start on Tuesday the thirteenth of May, which for a superstitious Englishman living in Spain, is not a good day to engage in anything that requires leaving the house, let alone the province.

I was to meet the producer at Malaga airport, after which, we would travel to Seville in a hire car supplied by the BBC.

The producer was a tall, wiry, bespectacled chap who more resembled a university professor, but he turned out to be an interesting fellow who had worked for the BBC for almost thirty years.

A senior producer for the BBC's religion and ethics department, he had worked a varied sphere of subjects including religious-themed topics in Afghanistan, Iran and China, to hip-hop documentaries in New York.

He was in Spain to record *'The spirit of flamenco',* an episode of BBC Radio Two's 'Guitar Season'; a series of programs based on the role of the guitar in the history of world music.

The documentary was also to focus on the role religion plays in flamenco, or more to the point, if it has any role at all!

There was also a priest to find; not just any priest, but one who was an aficionado of flamenco that would be willing to be questioned about flamenco and spirituality.

This was obviously going to be a little more difficult for me to organize, but I was astonished to be informed of a priest who would be delighted to participate.

The priest lived in Cordoba, and although I arranged the meeting, I did not partake in the interview, because my participation was confined to Seville and Utrera.

We arrived in Utrera in the early afternoon and the temperature had soared to 35º, and so we headed to a small bar opposite the hostel.

The appearance of two lofty Englishman intrigued the four or five undersized locals that were spread along the bar, but once the courteous *'holas'* had been exchanged, they soon returned to their conversations.

There are numerous small bars tucked away in the side streets of Utrera and they all rely totally on the custom of the local people, and for this reason, you will always be served good traditional local fare at a more than reasonable price.

They are basic cafes and are void of any ornamentation, and yet they are often so cheap to eat and drink in, one feels embarrassed when paying the bill.

After lunch we retired to the hostel for a short siesta, but there was little time for any shut-eye for me, because no sooner had my head hit the pillow, my phone began to buzz.

I had previously, but unsuccessfully, attempted to contact the people I had lined up for the interviews, but with the exception of Dani de Utrera, I could get no answer from any of them.

Dani had informed me that his habitual accompanist, Amador Gabarri, would not be able to assist, but I was not to worry, said he, because he had arranged another guitarist from Morón de la Frontera.

Although I assured the producer that everything was going to plan, I had still to find a location, and, of course, track down the absent artistes. Even though I have known these people for many years, I often forget that they are Andalusian gypsies, so there is often little chance of them arriving on time, if indeed at all.

But everything eventually went to plan, and so once the other artistes had been located, we set off to the center of the town, where I was to take the BBC on a quick tour of Utrera's flamenco hot-spots.

We wandered down the Calle Nueva and through the tiny back streets where so many flamencos had been born, or had previously lived. We then went to the beautiful bronze monument of La Fernanda and Bernarda de Utrera, and on to the small memorial park that honors many of the town's most celebrated artistes.

Whilst recording various bits and pieces in the park, the bells of the Santa Maria church began to clang, and this interruption gave me the idea of where we should interview the artistes and record the juerga; and what a wonderfully picturesque corner of Utrera this proved to be.

Andalusia is particularly beautiful in the spring, and the streets and plazas of Utrera were saturated with the aroma of differing blossom, and the purple flowers of the *Jacaranda* trees covered the floor like a carpet of confetti. The Santa Maria church became the backdrop for our documentary, and the small plaza opposite the church had the most perfect ambience for a little bit of gitanerias.

Luis el Marquesito and Dani de Utrera arrived looking fresh and keen to get started, but we awaited the arrival of the guitarist: he eventually appeared resembling the emblematic flamenco-dude; trilby hat, dark shades, and with his guitar thrown over his shoulder like a hunter's rifle.

Paco de Amparo, the great-nephew of the late Diego del Gastor, is part of one of the most important guitar dynasties in the history of flamenco, and he certainly possessed the same quality that his celebrated great-uncle once had.

Spirits were high, and the producer was anxious to get things started, and so he began giving instructions as to what it was he wanted them to do; which proved harder than the he had obviously expected.

One of the things the director had trouble coping with was the natural ambient of flamenco and he seemed concerned that he could not get silence when he thought he needed it.

He asked on several occasions for El Marquesito and Dani to refrain from interrupting with the jaleo whilst Paco was performing a solo piece on the guitar, but he eventually realized that this was not going to happen.

During a break in recording I informed him that if it was the 'authentic' form of this art that he was seeking, then he would find no better opportunity to capture it with his microphones.

He obviously wanted a crystal clear recording of the guitar, but what he actually canned was something far more astounding than he could have ever imagined.

The flamencos were relaxed and happy, which is a fine combination for a juerga, and after the initial interviews, they began to perform in the manner that I had hoped for.

The small plaza was soon reverberating with the wonderful voices of El Marquesito and Dani, and Paco's guitar sounded at its most beautiful during the recording of a buleria, when he incorporated the tolling of the church bells with the rhythm of his song.

Dani demonstrated why he is considered one of Utrera's most talented young flamenco singers, when he effortlessly recited a chilling saeta on the steps of the church: the sorrowful tone of his ghostly voice seemed to hover like a mist, which was then blasted away by the fury that rose from the soles of his feet and out of his mouth with the wrath of a demon.

El Marquesito was on fine form singing the cantes of his birthplace, and his face beamed with pride as he sang of his great-grandfather, the legendary 'Fernando El Pinini'.

As I stood in the wings watching these gypsies simply doing what comes so naturally to them, I felt content that we had indeed captured a little bit of Andalusian Gypsy magic.

As the sun set down behind the glowing Santa Maria church, and the microphones and equipment was neatly packed away in their chrome-cornered boxes, a sense of camaraderie prevailed.

These people are, without doubt, the most welcoming community I have ever encountered, and as we chatted and joked under the oranges trees in this attractive corner of the town, I was overcome with sentiment: I had set out to promote Utrera, and on this occasion, the Andalusian gypsies demonstrated the reason why I had taken the documentary to Utrera.

After the final photographs had been taken, and promises had been made, we all strolled down the hill to sample the delights of the bodega Doña Juana; all at the expense of the BBC of course.

FINAL SALUTATION

I have now lived in Andalusia for twenty years and in this time I have become addicted to so many of the features that this wonderful land has to offer, and it is a place which I now feel entitled to call my home.

I arrived in Andalusia a naive and somewhat uncultured young man, even though I believed that I was in fact culturally aware, and I soon began to discover that I had in actual fact led a somewhat sheltered existence for the past thirty years.

The first barrier came with the language, for I knew not one word of Spanish, other than 'gracias' and 'amigo'. I had been a bad student and had little interest in languages, and had even failed my French CSE, so I had no knowledge of any language other than English.

I feel that I must comment on the language because, although my Spanish has vastly improved since my first venture into Utrera, there are still times when I simply fail to connect with the conversation.

There are few rules within the Andalusian language and one can be easily confused because of the dialect that is used in the towns and villages of the south.

I am always confused by Spanish grammar and have often felt the need to apologize for my lack of it, but, unsurprisingly, not so many senior Andalusians have too greater need of it either.

The Andalusian language is a complex and confusing subject, and as with flamenco, knowledge is not necessarily an advantage over experience.

One may study the Spanish language or take lessons in order to speak, but one will often find that the dialect used in the streets and bars of Andalusia is somewhat alien to text-book Spanish.

There is a slang, or mixture of Gypsy and Andalusian, which bears little resemblance to Castilliano, and this, along with the quickness of the tongue, can sometimes confuse one beyond comprehension: of course, there are occasions when the locals are as mystified by my Spanish, as I theirs, especially during a noisy fiesta when the conversation is lost in the hullabaloo of the surroundings.

Along with the language barrier, I also found the food strange, the wine too strong, the cigarettes disgusting, the money confusing, and I certainly felt like a fish out of water: so why, one might ask, did I stay?

I had never before experienced such mystery, color and beauty as is attached to Southern Spain and I slowly became absolutely entangled in the turmoil of all things Andalusian. I began to acquire a taste for the local fables and legends that form much of this area's history, and I was captivated by the ambience of the romerias, the ferias and the hundreds of other colorful fiestas.

I was not overly religious, and knew nothing of the Catholic tradition, but I was soon caught in the claws of the Semana Santa celebrations, and it was much the same with the bullfight, because I was captivated by the kaleidoscope of color and the razzmatazz ambient; which incidentally, seems to surround all Andalusian traditions.

207

However, I must confess that the discovery of the Andalusian gypsies and their flamenco has been the chain that has imprisoned me in the very depths of southern Spain, because they seem to have affected my system like opium.

My introduction into the fabled world of flamenco has led me on an educational journey, which was to enlighten me with so many aspects of Spanish life, and I soon realized that the country in that, at first, I felt so alienated was beginning to consume me entirely.

I felt as if the soul of Andalusia was slowly seeping into my blood stream, but I soon realized that it was I that was slowing submerging into the abyss of this fertile land.

There are numerous villages and towns of great magnitude in Andalusia and most are crammed with historic architecture, picturesque plazas and romantic allegories, and although at first they may appear similar, each of these places has a distinctive character that sets it apart from the others.

The larger towns have become merged in the life of the modern world and have left behind the village orbit that allowed them to be self-sufficing, but Utrera has kept much of its idiosyncrasy.

I am forever excited about a visit to Utrera, and yet no matter what reason I have for going, the part that always excites me the most is simply being in the town.

The memories that I cherish most concerning my time in Utrera are often of every day happenings and are not exclusively to do with flamenco, and yet these simple incidents are what make Utrera so wonderfully attractive for me: of course there are numerous recollections of high-wired fiestas and drunken nights at the fair, but this is only a small part of what makes Utrera so pictorial.

A memorable incident happened during Easter one particular year, and it was a scene so magical, one felt that it had somehow been arranged.

It occurred during the 'night of the gypsies' and although this night is always a joyous occasion, I was particularly excited because I had received my first 'official' invitation to enter the church before the procession began.

There are two processions from the Santiago church on Maundy Thursday - El Silencio, and 'Los Gitanos' - and it was necessary to wait for the former to leave the church, before entry was permitted to the brotherhood of the gypsies.

I decided to watch the first procession before making good my invitation.

It was a beautiful moonlit night and there was not a cloud in the sky when the image of 'Christ the Captive' was shuffled through the huge portal of the church and set down at the top of the steep concrete steps. Much excitement was generated at the sight of this magnificent effigy, and the enthused spectators filled the air with cries of *viva el señor* and *guapo;* however, the mood elevated to a much greater high when a regiment of flamingos interlaced over head with the precision of a military flyover. This fabulous display created much emotion among the crowd and some, who no doubt believed it to be a sign, began muttering and crossing themselves in the distinctive Mediterranean catholic way.

Flamingos migrate mainly at night and they prefer to fly with a cloudless sky, and on this night their pink plumage shimmered in the star-studded sky as they veered overhead with gracious synchronized accuracy.

After two or three pass over's, they took off into the darkness of night, leaving the spectators in a state of wonderment, but as the image of Christ was hauled up into position, they appeared once again for a final salutation.

This surprise occurrence was really quite spectacular and it was one of those rare occasions when one sometimes questions ones belief.

A phrase I have often come across when discussing things of paranormal substance with a Spaniard, is that 'one does not need to see to believe; one must believe in order to see'. Spirituality plays a large role in the lives of most Andalusians and there are times when the unexplained, or situations such as this one, brings their saintly qualities racing to the surface.

One of the things I love most about these people is the simplicity that surrounds their existence and the quaintness in their attitude towards life in general: although some of them have tried to move with the times, many simply cannot, and in some cases, nor do they try to, understand anything unfamiliar to them.

Utrera is void of the tastelessness that has destroyed much of Andalusia's coastline, and one of the most appealing aspects is its daguerreotype characters.

Many of the older gypsies still dress in similar attire to what they did fifty years previous, and quite a few are illiterate, in so far as they cannot read or write; hence there are many that have not sufficiently adapted to the twenty-first century.

I am not suggesting that the gypsies are uneducated or naive, for the average Andalusian Gypsy is conversant with skills of the land and practiced in certain aspects of life that the non-Gypsy rarely encounters.

I speak mainly of the older generation, because their younger contemporaries have grasped the ways of the modern-world in which we now live, and although they still respect their traditions and customs, they are conversant with modern-day society and knowledgeable about world culture.

Andalusia has a literary elegance and its people are passionately lyrical, and one is often presented to a person who is said, or who claims, to be a poet, and although they will rarely have published anything, they seem to have a natural affection for the beauty of verse.

Andalusians are a people with a natural feeling for art and splendor, and their obsessive association with their *tierra* – the soil on which they were raised - is often the very substance of their art.

Although Utrera sits outside of flamenco's mythical 'golden triangle', it is densely interwoven with the areas of Jerez, Lebrija and Triana, and the clans of Gypsy flamencos from these places are approximating one entire family, and they all, with few exceptions, know how to perform the Gypsy art of flamenco.

One who is void of rhythm and unable to dance is considered something of an oddity, and those who do not know how to dance the sevillana are virtually unheard of; for this dance is allied to most aspects of their lives.

Birthdays, weddings, baptisms and any occasion that brings the whole family together will be accompanied by the twirling bodies and trotting rhythms of the sevillanas, and there is no sight more pleasurable than a room full of people engaging the harmonious routines of this dance.

The gypsies use the buleria in a similar way, and this spirited style of flamenco plays an integral part in any celebration, and everyone will sing, dance or simply clown around to the thumping of table tops and clapping of hands.

There is something quite regal about the buleria, and because it is always performed with such enthusiasm and gusto, it is the one style that best demonstrates the meaning of 'gitanerias'.

Memories of high-spirited fiestas, where the buleria becomes the epitome of the party, come flooding to mind whenever thinking of Utrera and, on occasions, the sheer radiance of the buleria will bring tears to my eyes.

Utrera has affected me in a way that I could never have before imagined, and although there are numerous other places with equal attraction, for me, Utrera will always remain the most majestic of them all.

Some of the most pleasurable occasions occurred during the feria and this has become the most important yearly entry in my diary, and an event that I refuse to pass up.

As I recall these moments and remember the wonderful times I have had in this town, I feel drenched in a sensation of complete enchantment. I feel somewhat privileged to be part of this great community and I am utterly grateful to have been accepted into the heart of their society; for they have shown me kindness and acceptance in a way that one cannot begin to comprehend.

As I bring this account of my time in Utrera to a conclusion, I am once again preparing to attend the wonderful feria in the town, and still today the mere thought of such pleasures sends adrenalin rushing through my body.

There is something about Utrera, and the way of life that exists there in, that makes a unique impression, and because the gypsies have lived there for more than five-centuries, it has a characteristic that is unlike any other.

Destiny will determine where I will end up next, although I am not convinced that I will ever experience the kind of reception that I have received in Utrera, but I feel comfortable with the feeling that it will be the gypsies and their music that will tempt me there.

GLOSSARY

Almohad

The Almohad dynasty ruled Andalusia during the 12th and early thirteenth centuries

Arabesque

Form of Islamic artistic decoration using intricately designed stucco

Azotea

Flat roof terrace

Ayuntamiento

Local Council

Bandolero

Bandits and highway-men of the eighteenth and nineteenth centuries

Banderillero

The torero who, on foot, places the harpoon tipped darts into the neck of the bull during the second act of the bullfight.

Barrera

The red painted fence that runs around the perimeter of the bullring: the first row of seats is known by the same name.

Botellón

Organized street parties

Brindi

The act of requesting permission to dedicate a bull to a personal friend or the entire crowd

Bulerías

Song style that occupies a supreme position in the world of flamenco because it is its most flexible and wide open to spontaneity; a truly majestic style of song and dance.

Burladero

Wooden shields set close together, behind which the bullfighter and his team can dodge if perused by the bull

Cabrón

Considered an ultimate insult if referring to a stranger, and yet it is also used in jest amongst friends

Cantiña

Song style that's name derives from the verb 'cantiñear', meaning improvised spontaneous song. The cantinas of Cadiz were gypsified and set to the rhythm of the alegrias, but in Jerez and Seville they developed more into the style of the buleria.

Cante

Flamenco song or singing

Caseta

Small make-shift marquee or hut used during the feria

219

Cateto

Rustic, villager, peasant

Cigarra

Cicada/treehopper

Cochero

Coachman

Cofradía

Brotherhood or fraternity

Compás

Rhythm or beat, but in flamenco depicts much more: if you have 'compás' then you will have good rhythm, character, knowledge and grace

Corrida

Bullfight

Costalero

Person that helps carry the images of the passion during Semana Santa

Cuadrilla

The matador's team or group

Falseta

Intricate guitar solos performed during the singers pauses

Feria

The fair

Fiesta

Party, celebration or 'one-day holiday' like Bank holiday

Fin de fiesta

End of the party; normally the final act of a flamenco recital where all present will dance a little 'buleria', before being led from the stage by the guitarist.

Gacho

Non-Gypsy

Ganadería

Farm where fighting bulls are bred and raised

221

Garrochista

Person who tests a bull's courage during the tienta: the garrochista is mounted on a horse and armed with a lance; with which he will attempt to assess the young animal's gallantry.

Gitano

Gypsy

Granadino

Person native of Granada

Hermandad

Brotherhood

Jaleo

Hell-raising: The encouragement of the artiste by the audience and the other performers

Juerga

Spontaneous flamenco session

Manzanilla

Strong Andalusian sherry.

Martinete

Old, unaccompanied, flamenco style that's origins are associated with the Gypsy blacksmiths

Mollete

Small flat bread roll native of Antequera, which is toasted and eaten at breakfast

Mudéjar

Name given to the Muslims of Al-Andaluz who remained in Spain after the Christian Reconquista

Muleta

The muleta is the red cloth that hides the sword used in the final act of the bullfight. The small cape is used to tire the bull and regulate the position of his head to aid the torero in the killing

Nazareno

Hooded penitents that assist the processions during Easter week

223

Novillero

Apprentice bullfighter

Palmas

Handclapping

Panda de Verdiales

Group of musicians and dancers that perform the verdiales

Paso

Floats that carry the images of the Passion in Seville

Pasodoble

Music typically played during bullfights; especially when the torero and his cuadro enter the ring, and during the faena, just before the kill

Peineta

Comb. Hair comb traditionally worn during Semana Santa and the feria

Peña

Club or private association

Picador

Torero with a lance that jabs the bull from horseback under the orders of the matador

Plaza

Square. Small square that is usually the center point of the community

Pringa

The meat of a stew, or the pringa, is removed and eaten separately and is often mashed together to form a mushy pulp. Pork, chorizo, black-pudding and chicken are mixed with olive oil, and either mashed with potatoes, or blended to form a thick paste.

Puchero

Chicken and vegetable stew

Romería

Pilgrimage. Procession held before most ferias, or pilgrimage that ends with a celebration at a shrine.

Romero

Rosemary. Its Spanish name means 'pilgrims plant'

Saeta

Style of unaccompanied singing usually reserved for Semana Santa

Semana Santa

Holy week

Sevillana

A colorful music and dance obligatory during the feria in Seville and the rest of Andalusia

Siguiriya

Gypsy flamenco style that is considered the very heart of all flamenco

Soleá

A song style at the heart of flamenco that's origins probably lie in Triana; with some of its best coming from Utrera and Alcalá de Guadaira

Tablao

A bar or club that presents flamenco in varying forms

Tertulia

Social gathering of a literary circle that takes place in a café or bar

Tienta

The tienta is the ceremony where young bulls are first tested to assess their courage: it is also one in which an aspiring matador can practice his art

Tío Pepe

Popular dry sherry from Jerez de la Frontera that is ever present during the feria

Torero

Bullfighter

Toro bravo

Literally 'brave bull' but refers to the fighting bull.

Trono

Floats that carry the images of the Passion in Málaga

Utreran

Person native of Utrera

228

By the same author

Flamenco; an Englishman's passion
Flamenco Heritage. The clan of El Pinini

www.tonybryant.searchgi.com

Printed in Great Britain
by Amazon